THE
resilience
JOURNAL

365 DAYS TO BALANCE
AND PEACE OF MIND

SANDRA E. JOHNSON

Clarkson Potter/Publishers

New York

We know what we want—ways to grow from adversities instead of being crushed by them; freedom from negative patterns of thinking and behaving; paths out of tumultuous suffering and into balance and peace. This journal is designed to help you develop these. For each day of the year, it offers inspirational quotes from people ranging from Buddha to don Miguel Ruiz to Oprah, followed by writing prompts to inspire you to create your own routes to resiliency.

Completing the daily prompts will build resiliency skills, one of which is the ability to respond positively to the only thing that is constant in life—**change**. Whether we want it to or not, everything—even the very planet we live on—is always changing. When we increase our acceptance of this it becomes easier to better appreciate good times and to recognize that tough times will eventually pass. Accepting change helps us slow down and resist the temptation to make rash, permanent decisions based upon impermanent circumstances. Instead, we can identify positive steps we can take while letting go of and moving past events we have no control over.

Another core component of resiliency is a clear perception of **reality**. *But I already have this*, you may say. But do you really? Misperception of reality is a common problem in our culture, such as the pervasive delusion that happiness comes only from buying the latest version of whatever, whether you need it or can afford it. Another illusion is that we are supposed to be doing something all the time—preferably several things at once—to the point where the mere idea of being still and quiet makes us nervous. Yet it is crucial to develop this capability so we can reconnect to the peace that is always within us. Just like if you dive deeply enough into an ocean you will find calm, if you dive deeply within yourself, you will find peace, the kind that helps you weather life's fiercest storms. And emerge stronger for it.

An additional building block for resilient living is understanding **we are not our thoughts** that our minds continually churn out because the nature of the mind is to think constantly, like the nature of the sea is to form waves. When we strengthen our skill to watch them like the surf as it ebbs and flows, their potential to sweep us away in worry, anger, sadness, and other uncentering emotions dissipates. We can ride them out, recognizing that just as they come, they go. We see who we really are beneath them instead of believing harsh self-judgments like "I'm stupid" when we make mistakes. We remain aware that we are intelligent people who make mistakes just because we are human.

Dozens of clinical studies prove that having **strong personal relationships** is another key component of resiliency. Having a good support system makes it easier to manage life's ups and downs. Research shows that people who have supportive family and friends tend to be happier, healthier, and live longer than those who isolate themselves.

Connection with nature enhances our resiliency, too. A 2015 Harvard study revealed that simply living in or near green spaces benefited research participants far beyond reducing their levels of depression, anxiety, and stress—it actually *prolonged* their lives. Living in spaces abundant with trees, plants, and other greenery reduced participants' risks of dying from respiratory illnesses by 34 percent and cut their risk of dying from cancer by 13 percent. In fact, living in such green spaces lowered people's risks of dying from *anything* other than accidents by a significant 12 percent. Though the vast majority of people in the study lived in urban areas, they enjoyed therapeutic areas in their yards, on their patios, terraces, or decks by surrounding themselves with plants and other greenery, demonstrating it does not take much to make a healing green space if you do not already have easy access to one.

Many studies by the National Institutes of Health and other research organizations prove that another core feature of resiliency is having a **consistent spiritual practice**. This goes far beyond the scope of organized religion. Indeed, many people find the most healing spiritual practice is regularly taking in the majesty of the natural world through everything from walking in a park, to fishing on a lake, or gazing at the sky. Meditation also provides a foundation for a spiritual practice. Some benefit from the traditional concept of sitting cross-legged with their eyes closed, but the act of focusing on nearly any kind of repetitive action—from breathing to biking—can be meditative. No matter which spiritual practice you choose, it is clear that regularly engaging in it tends to improve overall health and longevity while decreasing depression, anxiety, substance abuse, insomnia, and chronic pain.

The daily passages in this book incorporate each of the major components of resiliency in a format for you to integrate them more fully into your life. Doing so can assist you in reframing traumatic situations that have caused lingering distress. One of the many studies that proves this is by Susan Lutgendorf, PhD, with the University of Iowa. The participants in her project who wrote expressively about the most stressful times of their lives gained a greater understanding of how they benefited by surviving them than those in the control group who wrote about generic events. Such regular journaling also improves memory and other cognitive abilities and strengthens social skills.

The benefits are physical, too. The *Journal of the American Medical Association* reported research showing that four months after seventy patients with asthma and rheumatoid arthritis wrote twenty minutes for three consecutive days about the most stressful event of their lives, their lung functioning increased while their chronic pain decreased much more than patients in the project who only wrote about neutral happenings. The seventy patients also had less stress and were in better health than those in the control group. The psychologist who led the project, Joshua Smyth, PhD, said, "So writing helped patients get better, and also kept them from getting worse." If such major improvements came from journaling therapeutically *for only three days*, imagine the effects of doing so for *each of the 365 days* that *The Resilience Journal* covers.

In short, therapeutic writing is effective medicine you can use anytime, anywhere. So engage this book to forge your pathway to a life with much more resilience, balance, and peace of mind.

Initial Self-Assessment

To assess your current level of resilience, rate the following statements from 1 (strongly disagree) to 5 (strongly agree).

I cope well with frequent change.

| 1 | | 2 | | 3 | | 4 | | 5 |

I see problems as opportunities for personal growth.

| 1 | | 2 | | 3 | | 4 | | 5 |

It is easy for me to relax and focus on the present moment.

| 1 | | 2 | | 3 | | 4 | | 5 |

I am usually calm and centered.

| 1 | | 2 | | 3 | | 4 | | 5 |

I learn valuable lessons from every major setback I experience.

| 1 | | 2 | | 3 | | 4 | | 5 |

I meet most of the goals I set for myself.

| 1 | | 2 | | 3 | | 4 | | 5 |

I am a good problem solver.

| 1 | | 2 | | 3 | | 4 | | 5 |

I have a strong spiritual practice that helps keep me grounded.

| 1 | | 2 | | 3 | | 4 | | 5 |

I ask for help when I need it.

1 | 2 | 3 | 4 | 5

I seldom fret about situations I cannot control.

1 | 2 | 3 | 4 | 5

I treat myself with compassion.

1 | 2 | 3 | 4 | 5

I can quickly do things differently based upon new information.

1 | 2 | 3 | 4 | 5

I avoid using alcohol or other chemical substances to cope with stress.

1 | 2 | 3 | 4 | 5

I set aside time daily to rest, meditate, and reflect.

1 | 2 | 3 | 4 | 5

I have very supportive family and friends.

1 | 2 | 3 | 4 | 5

When things go wrong in my life, I typically take responsibility instead of blaming others.

1 | 2 | 3 | 4 | 5

I seldom dwell on negative thoughts or emotions.

1 | 2 | 3 | 4 | 5

I exercise regularly and maintain a healthy diet.

| 1 | 2 | 3 | 4 | 5 |

I have the skills I need to accomplish important goals.

| 1 | 2 | 3 | 4 | 5 |

Insignificant things seldom bother me.

| 1 | 2 | 3 | 4 | 5 |

I have hobbies that add to the quality of my life.

| 1 | 2 | 3 | 4 | 5 |

I feel good about myself.

| 1 | 2 | 3 | 4 | 5 |

I frequently draw comfort from nature.

| 1 | 2 | 3 | 4 | 5 |

I can stand up for myself when people try to mistreat me.

| 1 | 2 | 3 | 4 | 5 |

I face challenges head-on instead of just wishing they would go away.

| 1 | 2 | 3 | 4 | 5 |

Compare the number from this self-assessment with the one from the self-assessment you will do after completing this journal. While the optimal range is 100–125, any progress toward it is an encouraging sign that you increased your resilience.

Notes

What lies behind us and what lies before us are tiny matters compared to what lies within us. —RALPH WALDO EMERSON

Recount a time when you overcame a significant challenge. What did you learn from this experience?

_____

_____

_____

_____

_____

_____

_____

_____

_____

_____

_____

_____

_____

_____

_____

_____

_____

_____

The first step in this process of mindful awareness is radical self-acceptance. —STEPHEN BATCHELOR

We tend to be our worst critics. We focus on our shortcomings while ignoring our many good qualities. With this in mind, write at least five reasons to accept yourself just the way you are now.

_____

_____

_____

_____

_____

_____

_____

_____

_____

_____

_____

_____

_____

_____

_____

_____

_____

DAY 3

When you feel pain, simply view it as energy. Just start seeing these inner experiences as energy passing through your heart and before the eye of your consciousness. Then relax. —MICHAEL A. SINGER

Trying to fight emotional or physical pain tends to intensify it. To practice letting it move through you, find a quiet place where you can sit or lie comfortably for a few minutes. Next, take smooth, steady breaths as you imagine watching any negative sensations, thoughts, or feelings as if they were clouds passing across the sky of your mind, then journal about this experience.

_____

_____

_____

_____

_____

_____

_____

_____

_____

_____

_____

_____

_____

_____

Can you deal with the most vital matters by letting events take their course? —LAO TZU

Allowing events to unfold naturally instead of trying to contort them into how we think they should be makes for more peaceful, balanced living. Detail a time when you were able to do that and how you can apply those same skills in your life now.

_____

_____

_____

_____

_____

_____

_____

_____

_____

_____

_____

_____

_____

_____

_____

_____

_____

DAY
5

Joy is the holy fire that keeps our purpose warm and our intelligence aglow. —HELEN KELLER

What brings you joy and what are ways to bring more of it into your life?

_____

_____

_____

_____

_____

_____

_____

_____

_____

_____

_____

_____

_____

_____

_____

_____

_____

_____

If someone is not treating you with love and respect, it is a gift if they walk away from you. —DON MIGUEL RUIZ

Have you ever let go of an unhealthy relationship? If so, how did you do that? How can you apply those same skills to allow people who bring you more pain than happiness to transition out of your life?

_____

_____

_____

_____

_____

_____

_____

_____

_____

_____

_____

_____

_____

_____

_____

_____

_____

_____

_____

_____

_____

DAY
7

Spirituality is recognizing and celebrating that we are all inextricably connected to each other by a power greater than all of us, and that our connection to that power and to one another is grounded in love and compassion. Practicing spirituality brings a sense of perspective, meaning, and purpose to our lives. —BRENÉ BROWN, PhD

What does spirituality mean to you and how do you practice it?

_____

_____

_____

_____

_____

_____

_____

_____

_____

_____

_____

_____

_____

_____

_____

_____

_____

I was an exceptionally timid child, afraid of the dark, afraid of mice, afraid of practically everything. Painfully, step by step, I learned to stare down each of my fears, conquer it, attain the hard-earned courage to go on to the next. Only then was I really free. —ELEANOR ROOSEVELT

What fears have you conquered and how did you do it?

_____

_____

_____

_____

_____

_____

_____

_____

_____

_____

_____

_____

_____

_____

_____

_____

DAY 9

If I find a green meadow splashed with daisies and sit down beside a clear-running brook, I have found medicine. —DEEPAK CHOPRA, MD

Nature heals. Being outside also reminds us that we live in a world that is infinitely larger than any problems we could ever have, which helps put them in perspective. Go outside for about ten minutes, breathe mindfully as you take in everything around you in the natural world, then journal about how it felt.

_____

_____

_____

_____

_____

_____

_____

_____

_____

_____

_____

_____

_____

_____

_____

_____

_____

We find out what we really value in the daily decisions that we make, so we might do well to stop occasionally and respectfully ask ourselves: What truly matters? Asked regularly and fearlessly, it is the single question that will help you get to the heart of your life. —JAMES E. RYAN, JD

What truly matters to you? Does how you spend your time and money reflect that? If not, how might you change this?

_____

_____

_____

_____

_____

_____

_____

_____

_____

_____

_____

_____

_____

_____

Evoking the presence of the Great Compassion, let us fill our hearts with our own compassion—toward ourselves and toward all living beings.
—THICH NHAT HANH

How kind were you to yourself and others today? How might you be kinder?

Many of today's chronic illnesses, in particular heart disease and diabetes, have their roots in lifestyle choices, and they can also be alleviated by lifestyle choices. And there's nothing more powerful than choosing to eat clean and healthy food. —LAILA ALI

We would all benefit from being more conscious of *what* and *how* we eat. Start this journey into mindful eating with your favorite fresh fruit or vegetable. Use the space below to describe its color, texture, scent, and taste, and every sensation you experience while eating it.

DAY
13

Comfort kills, discomfort creates. —JEAN COCTEAU

Recount a circumstance that became so uncomfortable it forced you to make a significantly positive change. What skills did you use to make the change and how might you use them now?

_____

_____

_____

_____

_____

_____

_____

_____

_____

_____

_____

_____

_____

_____

_____

_____

_____

_____

_____

_____

Chaos is a friend of mine. —BOB DYLAN

Write about some chaos you experienced recently and your response to it.

_____

_____

_____

_____

_____

_____

_____

_____

_____

_____

_____

_____

_____

_____

_____

_____

_____

_____

DAY

15

What is your most important goal right now? What is the first step you need to take toward achieving it?

_____

_____

_____

_____

_____

_____

_____

_____

_____

_____

_____

_____

_____

_____

_____

_____

_____

_____

_____

_____

Creative adventures don't need to be fancy, groundbreaking, or even take a lot of time to be effective. In fact, simple acts of creative expression and innovation woven into daily life have an incredible way of soothing, stirring, and reminding us what it feels like to be alive. —FLORA BOWLEY

Practicing creativity helps build resiliency, so do something creative and journal about the experience.

DAY 17

If Plan A doesn't work, the alphabet has 25 more letters (204 if you're in Japan!). —CLAIRE COOK

Journal about a time you tried to reach a goal but did not and why. Was there another way to try? If so, what? Is it worth attempting now?

_____

_____

_____

_____

_____

_____

_____

_____

_____

_____

_____

_____

_____

_____

_____

_____

Now if there is nothing fearful for the elements themselves in their constant changing of each into another, why should one look anxiously in prospect at the change and dissolution of them all? This is in accordance with nature: and nothing harmful is in accordance with nature. —MARCUS AURELIUS

The only constant in life is change. What significant changes are you going through and what are they teaching you?

_____

_____

_____

_____

_____

_____

_____

_____

_____

_____

_____

_____

_____

_____

_____

_____

_____

DAY
19

Silence is the absolute poise or balance of body, mind, and spirit. —OHIYESA

Cultivating the ability to sit in silence helps to disconnect from stressors and reconnect with the peaceful center within. Sit in a quiet space while focusing on each inhalation and exhalation, then journal about this experience.

_____

_____

_____

_____

_____

_____

_____

_____

_____

_____

_____

_____

_____

_____

_____

_____

_____

_____

_____

_____

_____

Let Nature be your teacher. —WILLIAM WORDSWORTH

Take a short walk outside. What did you learn from it that might add to the quality of your life?

_____

_____

_____

_____

_____

_____

_____

_____

_____

_____

_____

_____

_____

_____

_____

_____

_____

DAY 21

If you see yourself as separate from everything outside of yourself, then there's potential to be in conflict with everything. There's no peace, no relaxation. When you start to free up unnecessary tension in your body and quiet the turmoil in your mind, the illusion of isolation lessens. —RODNEY YEE

Progressive relaxation is a useful technique to release tension. To practice this, find a place where you can lie comfortably and quietly. Take a few steady breaths and tighten your facial muscles for a moment, then allow them to soften while taking steady, full breaths. Repeat this process with your neck and shoulders and continue moving through the rest of your body. Record how you feel afterward.

_____

_____

_____

_____

_____

_____

_____

_____

_____

_____

_____

_____

_____

_____

_____

_____

_____

_____

People are like plants: they grow toward the light. —HOPE JAHREN, PhD

What sustains you? How can you incorporate more of it into your life?

DAY
23

Worry is a misuse of your imagination. —DAN ZADRA

What have you worried about recently and why? List more positive things you can focus on when you start worrying.

_____

_____

_____

_____

_____

_____

_____

_____

_____

_____

_____

_____

_____

_____

_____

_____

_____

_____

_____

_____

God is not found in the soul by adding anything, but by a process of subtraction. —MEISTER ECKHART

What can you subtract from your life to make more room for the Divine?

_____

_____

_____

_____

_____

_____

_____

_____

_____

_____

_____

_____

_____

_____

_____

_____

_____

_____

DAY
25

What are a few of the most important lessons you have learned so far that have lightened your life?

_____

_____

_____

_____

_____

_____

_____

_____

_____

_____

_____

_____

_____

_____

_____

_____

_____

_____

_____

_____

When you stand and share your story in an empowering way, your story will heal you and your story will heal somebody else. —IYANLA VANZANT

Write about a time when you told someone about a hard time you survived, and you both felt better for it.

_____

_____

_____

_____

_____

_____

_____

_____

_____

_____

_____

_____

_____

_____

_____

_____

_____

_____

_____

_____

_____

The power of clarity is not that the anger won't arise, because it will. It's so we can make the most considered, compassionate response. —SYLVIA BOORSTEIN

What has recently angered you? What typically angers you? Next time you're in a similar situation, how can you respond in a more constructive manner?

_____

_____

_____

_____

_____

_____

_____

_____

_____

_____

_____

_____

_____

_____

_____

_____

_____

_____

_____

_____

_____

I am not what happened to me. I am what I choose to become. —CARL JUNG

What are you choosing to become and why? What is helping you? Is anything hindering you? If so, what can you do about it?

_____

_____

_____

_____

_____

_____

_____

_____

_____

_____

_____

_____

_____

_____

_____

_____

_____

_____

_____

_____

DAY
29

When this world upsets me, this music sets me free. —GARY CLARK JR.

When this world upsets you, what sets you free?

_____

_____

_____

_____

_____

_____

_____

_____

_____

_____

_____

_____

_____

_____

_____

_____

_____

_____

_____

Sometimes we have to look really deeply and pay close attention to finding beauty because it doesn't seem to be there. But it is. And it's imperative that we never stop searching for it. —JENNIFER PASTILOFF

Where do you look for beauty to enhance the quality of your life? Where else might you find it?

_____

_____

_____

_____

_____

_____

_____

_____

_____

_____

_____

_____

_____

_____

_____

_____

DAY
31

If you want to know others,
begin by knowing yourself,
because
everyone is a mirror. —LOUIS CLAUDE DE SAINT-MARTIN

What do you know that is most true about yourself?

_____

_____

_____

_____

_____

_____

_____

_____

_____

_____

_____

_____

_____

_____

_____

_____

_____

_____

Our technological society has convinced us to stay in touch, but not with ourselves. —JULIA CAMERON

On average, how much time each day do you spend using your phone, computer, smart watch, and TV? Does it allow you enough time for quiet self-reflection and contemplation? If not, specify parameters for using these devices.

_____

_____

_____

_____

_____

_____

_____

_____

_____

_____

_____

_____

_____

_____

_____

_____

DAY 33

At a certain point, it doesn't really matter so much how we got to be a certain way. Until we admit our character defects—and take responsibility for the fact that regardless of where we got them, they are ours now ... [they] won't go away. —MARIANNE WILLIAMSON

What is your most significant character defect? What are constructive ways to address it?

I have found that among its other benefits, giving liberates the soul of the giver. —MAYA ANGELOU

How do you give to others and how do you usually feel afterward?

_____

_____

_____

_____

_____

_____

_____

_____

_____

_____

_____

_____

_____

_____

_____

_____

_____

_____

_____

_____

_____

Also our Lord God showed
that it is full great pleasure to Him
that a pitiable soul come to Him nakedly and plainly and simply.
For this is the natural yearning of the soul. —JULIAN OF NORWICH

It takes mindfulness to strengthen the ability to be still and silent enough to reconnect to ourselves and our Higher Power.

Find a place where you can rest comfortably in silence. Stay there as long as you need, then journal about the experience.

_____

_____

_____

_____

_____

_____

_____

_____

_____

_____

_____

_____

_____

_____

_____

_____

Most chaos is a product of some past, oftentimes imagined slight. One way to free yourself from this chaos is to try to stay present in the moment, to not layer an experience with the emotions of memorable chaotic past experiences as well. —KAREN CASEY, PhD

Breath work can center you in the present moment. One variation of this is alternate nostril breathing. Find a quiet location and position yourself comfortably. Next, take a full breath in, then gently press your thumb to close off your right nostril while slowly releasing your breath through the left one. At the end of the breath, press your ring finger against the left nostril while inhaling through the right one.

Repeat this process for several minutes, concentrating as best you can on inhaling through one nostril, and exhaling from the other. Now journal about how you feel.

_____

_____

_____

_____

_____

_____

_____

_____

_____

_____

_____

_____

_____

DAY 37

It is as easy to forget
Everything that matters as
It is easy to lose a mountain to the sky. —LAURA HOPE-GILL

What is most important to you? Does your lifestyle reflect it? If not, why and what
are your options for changing this?

_____

_____

_____

_____

_____

_____

_____

_____

_____

_____

_____

_____

_____

_____

_____

_____

_____

_____

We recognize that we must find deep inner strength so we don't get destroyed by the waves that come and try to toss us around. —KRISHNA DAS

How do you best connect with your deep inner strength? What other ways might you try?

_____

_____

_____

_____

_____

_____

_____

_____

_____

_____

_____

_____

_____

_____

_____

_____

_____

_____

_____

We have to protect our mind and our body, rather than just go out there and do what the world wants us to do. —SIMONE BILES

Journal about a time when you defied what others wanted you to do in order to take care of yourself and then a time that you did the opposite. What lessons do these experiences offer?

_____

_____

_____

_____

_____

_____

_____

_____

_____

_____

_____

_____

_____

_____

_____

_____

_____

_____

_____

Our life is frittered away by detail. . . . Simplify, simplify.
—HENRY DAVID THOREAU

How can you simplify your life?

_____

_____

_____

_____

_____

_____

_____

_____

_____

_____

_____

_____

_____

_____

_____

_____

_____

_____

_____

_____

_____

When you write books, you meet challenges. I saw so many writers paralyzed by failure, but also by success. They wrote one successful book, and then they stopped writing. —PAULO COELHO

Has reaching one goal ever left you stuck at a plateau toward achieving a higher one? If so, write about the occurrence and what you can learn from it.

_____

_____

_____

_____

_____

_____

_____

_____

_____

_____

_____

_____

_____

_____

_____

_____

_____

It's important that we don't trivialize the word prayer *by turning it into simply a means to get what we want. . . . We should consider* prayer *the umbrella word for* all the interior journeys or practices that allow us to experience faith, hope, and love. —RICHARD ROHR

Use the space below to write a prayer about whatever is on your mind and in your soul.

_____

_____

_____

_____

_____

_____

_____

_____

_____

_____

_____

_____

_____

_____

_____

_____

_____

_____

DAY 43

You think your pain and your heartbreak are unprecedented in the history of the world, but then you read. It was books that taught me that the things that tormented me most were the very things that connected me with all the people who were alive, or who had ever been alive. —JAMES BALDWIN

Which books have helped you feel less alone and why? Which others can you read for this same purpose?

_____

_____

_____

_____

_____

_____

_____

_____

_____

_____

_____

_____

_____

_____

_____

_____

_____

The universe will bring you an abundance of opportunities and possibilities. It's really all about trusting that before you got there, when you were sleeping, the universe was conspiring to give you something to blow your mind. Would you be open to receive it? —CARLOS SANTANA

Remember a time when you received an unexpected but wonderful opportunity. How did you respond to it? How can you become more open to similar opportunities?

_____

_____

_____

_____

_____

_____

_____

_____

_____

_____

_____

_____

_____

_____

_____

_____

When things fall apart and we're on the verge of we know not what, the test for each of us is to stay on that brink and not concretize. —PEMA CHÖDRÖN

No matter how we try to prevent it, things fall apart. The question is not *will* things go wrong, but *when*. But *we choose* how to respond to this inevitability.

Remembering how you survived difficult times in the past helps reinforce your resiliency when facing challenging times now and in the future. Write about such a time and how you overcame it.

_____

_____

_____

_____

_____

_____

_____

_____

_____

_____

_____

_____

_____

_____

_____

_____

*Therapy isn't a waste of time. It can save a friendship, a marriage,
a life.* —MARIA SHRIVER

Is there a painful issue that you have not been able to resolve on your own
that is interfering with the quality of your life? Would therapy help? If so, create
a plan to get it.

_____

_____

_____

_____

_____

_____

_____

_____

_____

_____

_____

_____

_____

_____

_____

_____

_____

The way I go to church is to go to the woods. —BARBARA KINGSOLVER

Some people's favorite "church" is a lush forest, a quiet beach, or even their own backyard. Where do you go to honor and celebrate all that is sacred?

_____

_____

_____

_____

_____

_____

_____

_____

_____

_____

_____

_____

_____

_____

_____

_____

_____

_____

_____

_____

I remind myself, "Don't let the perfect be the enemy of the good."... A twenty-minute walk that I do is better than the four-mile run that I don't do. The imperfect book that gets published is better than the perfect book that never leaves my computer. The dinner party of take-out Chinese food is better than the elegant dinner that I never host. —GRETCHEN RUBIN

How comfortable are you with imperfection? What can help increase your comfort level?

_____

_____

_____

_____

_____

_____

_____

_____

_____

_____

_____

_____

_____

_____

_____

_____

So after having a double mastectomy by the time I was forty-three, where is the bright side?

First I noticed that I was noticing my life. It was as if someone had stood next to me in the supermarket line and yelled in my ear, in the loudest voice imaginable—"Wake up!!!!" I stopped sleepwalking through my days. I started paying attention. —HILENE FLANZBAUM

What trauma have your survived that is making you pay more attention to your life?

Mindfulness is like a flood light, shining awareness on the whole field of experience including sensations, emotions, and thoughts as they arise and pass away in the dynamic, ever-changing flux that characterizes the human experience of body and mind. —FRANK JUDE BOCCIO

Take a few steady breaths, then note what you are most aware of at this moment.

_____

_____

_____

_____

_____

_____

_____

_____

_____

_____

_____

_____

_____

_____

_____

_____

_____

_____

Do your little bit of good where you are; it's those little bits of good put together that overwhelm the world. —DESMOND TUTU

What little bit of good can you do within the next twenty-four hours?

_____

_____

_____

_____

_____

_____

_____

_____

_____

_____

_____

_____

_____

_____

_____

_____

_____

_____

_____

_____

Hindsight is always 20/20. But we have to live our lives facing forward, without benefit of knowing how it will all turn out, and we have to have mercy for ourselves for not being fortune-tellers. That's why I've always seen regret as a particularly torturous capacity of our minds. What good does it do to beat ourselves up for things we couldn't have known at the time? We did the best we could with what we had. —M. J. RYAN

What is a regret you can let go of, knowing that you made the best decision you could at the time with what you knew then?

_____

_____

_____

_____

_____

_____

_____

_____

_____

_____

_____

_____

_____

_____

_____

_____

DAY 53

I tell my students one of the most important things they need to know is when they are their best, creatively. They need to ask themselves, What does the ideal room look like? Is there music? Is there silence? Is there chaos outside or is there serenity outside? What do I need in order to release my imagination? —TONI MORRISON

Describe the setting in which you are most creative and what it is about it that nourishes your creativity.

_____

_____

_____

_____

_____

_____

_____

_____

_____

_____

_____

_____

_____

_____

_____

_____

_____

_____

_____

You can't possibly assume you know someone just because of a demographic,
like religion or race. People are beautiful mysteries. —LAUREN VOGELBAUM

Recall one time that you made a false assumption about someone based on
something like religion or race and then a time that someone did the same to you.
What did you learn from these two occurrences?

_____

_____

_____

_____

_____

_____

_____

_____

_____

_____

_____

_____

_____

_____

_____

_____

DAY
55

Perhaps the type of refuge you've most longed for is that from the tyranny of your mind. If you meditate, you know too well how powerful the constant barrage of arising thoughts can be. But meditation can help you create refuge in the midst of your mind. —JUDITH LASATER, PhD

Try a movement meditation to quiet your thoughts. Sway gently from side to side, perhaps to relaxing instrumental music, while repeating a calming phrase, such as "It will be okay." Do this for five to ten minutes, then journal about how you feel.

_____

_____

_____

_____

_____

_____

_____

_____

_____

_____

_____

_____

_____

_____

_____

_____

_____

_____

Over the course of your adulthood, you develop your own tools, and for me, it's turning off the noise that is upsetting. —MICHELLE OBAMA

What are effective tools you have found to reduce stress? What others might you try?

_____

_____

_____

_____

_____

_____

_____

_____

_____

_____

_____

_____

_____

_____

_____

_____

_____

_____

_____

DAY
57

When you pray, move your feet. —AFRICAN PROVERB

What are you doing to help make what you pray for become reality?

_____

_____

_____

_____

_____

_____

_____

_____

_____

_____

_____

_____

_____

_____

_____

_____

_____

_____

_____

_____

If we really want to live a joyful, connected, and meaningful life, we must *talk about things that get in the way.* —BRENÉ BROWN, PhD

What interferes with your ability to have a joyful, connected, and meaningful life and what can you do about it?

_____

_____

_____

_____

_____

_____

_____

_____

_____

_____

_____

_____

_____

_____

_____

_____

_____

_____

DAY 59

I could not say certain sounds, like r, so I would be saying things like poetwee or dolla. My last name is Gorman, and I could not say that really until three years ago. For a long time, I looked at it as a weakness. Now I really look at it as a strength because going through that process, it made me a writer, for one, because I had to find a form in which I could communicate other than through my mouth, and two, when I was brave enough to try to take those words from the page onto the stage, I brought with me this understanding of the complexity of sound, pronunciation, emphasis. —AMANDA GORMAN

What is a weakness that, as you look back on it, actually helped you?

_____

_____

_____

_____

_____

_____

_____

_____

_____

_____

_____

_____

_____

_____

*Spirituality is freeing because it means opening the heart and doing your
darnedest to see every nanosecond of existence through this aperture.
Always, you must ask, "How can a situation—any situation—help me grow
and develop loving-kindness toward myself and others?" Both with patients
and personally, I've seen the authority this question has to recast despair.*
—JUDITH ORLOFF, MD

Recall a situation that helped you to grow and develop loving-kindness toward
yourself and others.

_____

_____

_____

_____

_____

_____

_____

_____

_____

_____

_____

_____

_____

_____

_____

DAY
61

Once you have experienced what it's like to have a truly ordered house, you'll feel your whole world brighten. —MARIE KONDO

How organized is your home? Is it possible to bring more order to it and thus bring more peace into your life? If so, use the space below to develop a plan to do this.

_____

_____

_____

_____

_____

_____

_____

_____

_____

_____

_____

_____

_____

_____

_____

_____

_____

_____

We all wear scars—find someone who makes yours feel beautiful. —ATTICUS

Who makes your scars feel beautiful and how do they do that?

_____

_____

_____

_____

_____

_____

_____

_____

_____

_____

_____

_____

_____

_____

_____

_____

_____

_____

DAY
63

For this is the cause why we be not all in ease of heart and soul . . . [that we]
seek here rest, in these things that are so little wherein is no rest, and know
not our God who is all mighty, all wise, all good. For he is the very rest.
—JULIAN OF NORWICH

Though Julian of Norwich wrote those words in the fourteenth century, they are more relevant now than ever because of how our culture encourages us to seek rest in things that ultimately cause anguish.

Do you sometimes seek rest in things or actions that offer temporary relief but eventually stress you? If so, what are they? What can you replace them with to improve your well-being?

---

*We tend to stick to our habits, even the ones that cause us to suffer.
Workaholism is one example. In the past, our ancestors may have had
to work nearly all the time to put food on the table. But today, our way of
working is rather compulsive and prevents us from having real contact
with life.* —THICH NHAT HANH

What is the quality of your work-life balance? If it is something you want to
change, use the space below to create an action plan to do so.

_____

_____

_____

_____

_____

_____

_____

_____

_____

_____

_____

_____

_____

_____

_____

_____

When the Nameless One debuts again
Ten thousand facets of my being unfurl wings
And reveal such a radiance inside
I enter a realm divine—
I too begin to so sweetly cast light,
Like a lamp,
Through the streets of this
World. —HAFIZ

How have you recently cast the light within you to others?

_____

_____

_____

_____

_____

_____

_____

_____

_____

_____

_____

_____

_____

_____

The single best way to improve our well-being is to show kindness
toward ourselves and others. Since most of us have more difficulty
with the former, I recommend that you focus first on graduating from
self-criticism. —MARTHA BECK

What do you tend to criticize yourself for? How might you develop a more
compassionate attitude toward yourself about this?

_____

_____

_____

_____

_____

_____

_____

_____

_____

_____

_____

_____

_____

_____

_____

_____

_____

DAY
67

Insanity is repeating the same mistakes and expecting different results.
—NARCOTICS ANONYMOUS

Have you repeated an action—either consciously or unconsciously—expecting it to produce different results? If so, what is it? Just increasing your awareness about this can help you avoid repeating it.

_____

_____

_____

_____

_____

_____

_____

_____

_____

_____

_____

_____

_____

_____

_____

_____

_____

_____

*"Look how he abused me and
beat me,
How he threw me down and robbed
me."
Live with such thoughts and you live
in hate.* —BUDDHA

It is a fine line between acknowledging wrongs done to you and dwelling
on them, allowing them to profoundly affect you. How well do you strike this
balance? If you need therapy for this, develop a plan to access it.

_____

_____

_____

_____

_____

_____

_____

_____

_____

_____

_____

_____

_____

_____

_____

_____

_____

DAY 69

You have to ask, what is it that really activates the spirit within me? For one person, it will be working with their hands; for another person, it's a creative endeavor; for another, it's an intellectual activity. It's different for all of us. —JAMES HOLLIS, PhD

What activates the spirit within you? How might you integrate this more into your life?

_____

_____

_____

_____

_____

_____

_____

_____

_____

_____

_____

_____

_____

_____

_____

_____

_____

I'm wiser and I know how to handle success now. But success has different meanings to me. When someone comes up to me and says, "I was a dropout in school and I heard your song 'You Can Get It If You Really Want,' and that song made me go back to school, and now I am a teacher and I use your song with my students."—that, for me, is a big success. —JIMMY CLIFF

What accomplishment have you achieved that, in reflecting on it, was more important than you originally thought?

_____

_____

_____

_____

_____

_____

_____

_____

_____

_____

_____

_____

_____

_____

_____

_____

DAY 71

I opened my business with one KitchenAid mixer and a dorm-size refrigerator. I didn't have any credit or money. I was sitting in the back of my house with no electricity, living on a generator, and counting my dollars trying to do something different. I had $5 left when my neighbor knocked on the door and asked to place an order. —MIGNON FRANCOIS

Since that grim day in 2008, Mignon Francois went on to open a bakery in Nashville that has sold more than five million sweet delights and garnered national acclaim. No matter how bleak your circumstances are, it can take only one small action—in her case, a neighbor placing an order—to start turning things around.

What small action turned things around for you during a low time or has the potential to do so now?

_____

_____

_____

_____

_____

_____

_____

_____

_____

_____

_____

_____

_____

_____

Many of your fears are rooting in physical actions or things: heights, swimming, standing or speaking in front of large crowds. If we conquer those types of fears through adventure—hiking up mountains, scuba diving, etc.—we can conquer anything. —CHRISTINA RICE

Do you have a fear that holds you back in some significant way? If so, develop a plan to begin to conquer it through some type of adventure.

_____

_____

_____

_____

_____

_____

_____

_____

_____

_____

_____

_____

_____

_____

_____

_____

_____

_____

DAY
73

We decide. That's the revelation. We decide if we are going to live lives that are bitter or sweet. We decide, in every moment, to respond from peace or from fear. We decide. —KAREN CASEY, PhD

Recount a difficult situation in which you responded with peace instead of fear. How were you able to do that? How might you apply that same ability to current challenges?

_____

_____

_____

_____

_____

_____

_____

_____

_____

_____

_____

_____

_____

_____

_____

_____

_____

With training, every time we breathe in and out, mindfulness will be there, so that our breathing becomes a cause and condition for arising on mindfulness. —THICH NHAT HANH

Conscious breathing is a key component of developing and sustaining mindfulness. Focusing on our breath shifts our attention from the chaos that can swirl around us and in our own minds and helps us to reconnect to the deep peace within.

Settle someplace where you will not be disturbed for at least ten minutes. Next, breathe in fully and steadily, taking a moment to pause at the end of each inhalation and exhalation. Try to pay close attention to each breath. When your attention wanders—which it will because that is the nature of the mind—simply refocus it on your breath. Next, write how you feel.

_____

_____

_____

_____

_____

_____

_____

_____

_____

_____

_____

_____

_____

*Care about people's approval
and you will be their prisoner.* —LAO TZU

From the time we enter this world, most of us are conditioned to seek the approval of others. This "need to please" can be shackling, preventing us from being our authentic selves. Is this an issue for you? If so, whose approval do you seek and how might you let go of this habit?

_____

_____

_____

_____

_____

_____

_____

_____

_____

_____

_____

_____

_____

_____

_____

_____

_____

What keeps you alive and how?

And hard times come, and hard times go.
And hard times come, and hard times go.
And hard times come, and hard times go. —BRUCE SPRINGSTEEN

When we are experiencing difficult situations, it is easy to fall into the delusion that they will go on forever, but they will not, if for no reason other than the fact that everything in existence has a beginning, middle, and end, and challenging circumstances are no exception.

Use the space below to journal about a difficult time in your life that you thought would never end but ultimately did.

We are urgently rushing toward some goal or dream, or an ever-elusive "finish line" of some sort. Under the pretense of pursuing happiness (and the heavy weight of questions like "Where do you see yourself five years from now?"), we imagine a different version of ourselves existing in the distant future somewhere—often richer, calmer, stable and wise.

As a result, we spend very little time appreciating where we are today. By being so focused on how things "could be," we are under-appreciating how great things already are. —TIMBER HAWKEYE

What is good in your life right now?

_____

_____

_____

_____

_____

_____

_____

_____

_____

_____

_____

_____

_____

_____

I like to take the time to listen to the trees, much in the same way that I listen to a sea shell, holding my ear against the rough bark of the trunk, hearing the inner singing of the sap. It's a lovely sound, the beating of the heart of a tree. —MADELEINE L'ENGLE

When we shift our focus to the natural world, it helps us turn our attention from regrets about the past and worries about the future to the gift that is the present moment. Take this journal outside for about ten minutes and concentrate on the sounds you hear in nature—from birdsong to wind moving through the trees—then describe how you feel as a result of this activity.

_____

_____

_____

_____

_____

_____

_____

_____

_____

_____

_____

_____

_____

_____

_____

_____

Have a variety of interests. . . . These interests relax the mind and lessen the tension on the nervous system. People with many interests live, not only longest, but happiest. —GEORGE MATTHEW ALLEN

What are your interests and why? Do you have enough of them? If not, how might you change this?

_____

_____

_____

_____

_____

_____

_____

_____

_____

_____

_____

_____

_____

_____

_____

_____

_____

_____

_____

DAY 81

But the real antidote to the discomfort of uncertainty is to move into it rather than away from it. You connect to the way the discomfort feels in your body. You let yourself feel it. You let go of the story that inevitably accompanies feelings of discomfort. And you just stay present with yourself with your feelings, without resistance or expectation. The more you can be present with uncertainty, the more you can let the change process take place naturally and effectively. —SALLY KEMPTON

To practice staying present through discomfort, set aside ten minutes or so in a quiet place, close your eyes, and breathe mindfully, just noticing any sensations and allowing them to move through your awareness, like breezes passing by. Then journal about this experience.

_____

_____

_____

_____

_____

_____

_____

_____

_____

_____

_____

_____

_____

I've learned that making a "living" is not the same as "making a life."
—MAYA ANGELOU

Is making a living interfering with your ability to make a meaningful life? If so, create an action plan with specific objectives and target dates for changing this.

_____

_____

_____

_____

_____

_____

_____

_____

_____

_____

_____

_____

_____

_____

_____

_____

I never thought I'd be a yoga teacher. I got forced into teaching my first class by my father, who was leaving town and wanted me to substitute.... During that class I tapped into something in myself. I saw that people authentically enjoyed it, and it touched something in me. My father said, "You know a lot, and you've grown up around a lot of great teachers. If you don't share what you know, you lose it. You have a responsibility."

Those words combined with that first teaching experience resonated with me. He pushed me over the cliff, and instead of falling, I flew. —BARON BAPTISTE

What experience pushed you beyond your perceived limits in a way that greatly benefited you and others?

Cultivate the willingness to love your judging mind instead of fighting it.
This is very powerful. Taking time to be quiet and aware can help us see
clearly that we live with a constant and unremitting critical mind. We judge
ourselves with ferocity, and we judge others without surcease. It's a radical
practice to notice this and actually contemplate the opposite—loving the
humanness of our judging mind. This is a form of self-care that is especially
liberating. —JUDITH LASATER, PhD

Identify something about yourself or others that you judge that you can be more
compassionate about rather than battling it.

_____

_____

_____

_____

_____

_____

_____

_____

_____

_____

_____

_____

_____

_____

DAY 85

A thought is harmless unless we believe it. It's not our thoughts, but the attachment to our thoughts, that causes suffering. —BYRON KATIE

Do you have unsettling thoughts that you tend to believe simply because your mind generates them? If so, what are they? Just being more conscious of them can lessen their impact on you.

_____

_____

_____

_____

_____

_____

_____

_____

_____

_____

_____

_____

_____

_____

_____

_____

_____

_____

It's up to us to stay curious, to keep evolving, and to let go of what no longer serves us. —LIZ CLARK

What no longer serves you or perhaps never did? How might you let go of it?

_____

_____

_____

_____

_____

_____

_____

_____

_____

_____

_____

_____

_____

_____

_____

_____

_____

_____

_____

_____

DAY 87

When we accept life as it is, dissatisfaction and suffering cease, and we learn to deal with reality on its own terms, rather than what our minds desire. —RICHARD MILLER, PhD

What is a reality in your life that is hard to accept? Just bringing it to your awareness can be the starting point of accepting it.

_____

_____

_____

_____

_____

_____

_____

_____

_____

_____

_____

_____

_____

_____

_____

_____

_____

Only in feeling my sadness can I learn from it and deepen through it. My sadness is often my teacher, as I learn to outgrow its causes within myself.
—MARIANNE WILLIAMSON

What are sources of sadness for you? What can they teach you?

_____

_____

_____

_____

_____

_____

_____

_____

_____

_____

_____

_____

_____

_____

_____

_____

_____

_____

Often when we find ourselves in a difficult situation we come to believe we have no options. We convince ourselves there is no way out. Despair and frustration take root and convince us that things are more desperate than they may actually be. When I've found myself in those situations in my own life, I have learned that a change in perspective can change everything. What seems insurmountable can be overcome. Not without difficulty, but through ingenuity and dedication. —SUZE ORMAN

Recount a time when changing your perspective about a difficult dilemma helped you resolve it. How did you transform your thoughts about the issue? How might you apply that skill to other problems?

_____

_____

_____

_____

_____

_____

_____

_____

_____

_____

_____

_____

_____

Often we're only partially paying attention to someone's response because we're busy thinking of what we want to say next. —JAMES E. RYAN, JD

Detail a time when you fully focused on another person's response and another time when you concentrated more on what you would say afterward. What made the differences between these two events? How might you be more present during challenging conversations so you can truly hear what the other person is telling you?

_____

_____

_____

_____

_____

_____

_____

_____

_____

_____

_____

_____

_____

_____

_____

_____

DAY 91

*Do you have the patience to wait
till your mud settles and the water is clear?
Can you remain unmoving
till the right action arises by itself?* —LAO TZU

Recall a time when you resisted the urge to immediately react to a difficult situation and waited until you understood it more clearly. Did this help you make a better decision about what to do? How were you able to resist the urge and how can you use that same ability going forward?

_____

_____

_____

_____

_____

_____

_____

_____

_____

_____

_____

_____

_____

_____

_____

It doesn't matter how your life has unfolded up to this moment. I want you to remember this: every single morning, you open your eyes and win the megamillion-dollar lottery of being alive. With each second of the day, you are given 86,400 chances to choose differently than you have in the past. —PANACHE DESAI

Is there a choice you can make today that is different from ones you have made in the past that can help you, even if in a small way? If so, what is it?

_____

_____

_____

_____

_____

_____

_____

_____

_____

_____

_____

_____

_____

_____

_____

_____

The seeking, with faith, hope, and charity, pleaseth our Lord, and finding pleaseth the soul and fulfilleth it with joy. —JULIAN OF NORWICH

How do you seek the Divine? What additional ways might you do this?

_____

_____

_____

_____

_____

_____

_____

_____

_____

_____

_____

_____

_____

_____

_____

_____

_____

_____

_____

I have cancer but I also have windy summer mornings in the rain and an active sense of awe at all that I can still touch and taste and see and hear and breathe in at any given moment. —LILA KEARY

Which precious things do you still have despite challenges in your life?

_____

_____

_____

_____

_____

_____

_____

_____

_____

_____

_____

_____

_____

_____

_____

_____

_____

DAY 95

Isvara is a distinct, incorruptible form of pure awareness, utterly independent of cause and effect and lacking any store of latent impressions. . . . Isvara is represented by the sound om. *Through repetition its meaning becomes clear. Then interiorization develops and obstacles fade away.*
—PATANJALI

Chanting a short word, such as *om*—which represents pure consciousness—is one way to calm our often wild minds and reduce stress. Go somewhere that you will not be disturbed for at least ten minutes. Begin consciously breathing, then with each full exhalation, chant whichever word you have selected, focusing on the sound as it vibrates through your body and into spaciousness. Then journal how you feel.

_____

_____

_____

_____

_____

_____

_____

_____

_____

_____

_____

_____

_____

_____

What do sad people have in common?
It seems they have all built a shrine to the past
And often go there and do a strange wail and worship. —HAFIZ

On a separate sheet of paper, write about something from your past that continues to trouble you. Next burn the paper, reducing it to ash. Once the ash is cool, dispose of it in a way that helps you let go of that part of your past. Finally, journal about this exercise.

_____

_____

_____

_____

_____

_____

_____

_____

_____

_____

_____

_____

_____

_____

DAY
97

All that is required to become free of the ego is to be aware of it, since awareness and ego are incompatible. —ECKHART TOLLE

Journal about a time when you allowed your ego to get the best of you. What did you learn from this?

_____

_____

_____

_____

_____

_____

_____

_____

_____

_____

_____

_____

_____

_____

_____

_____

_____

_____

Have we established that questions are marvelous, momentous things? And if so, can we agree that asking ourselves the right ones can have life-altering effects? Because have you ever noticed how questions prevent us from settling for less than we deserve? That asking ourselves Could it be better? *is a great way to make things, well, a whole lot better? That a bunch of our breakthroughs, triumphs, and joys occurred when we asked a few big, bold, paradigm-shifting questions?* —KATIE ARNOLD-RATLIFF

What is a question you asked yourself that changed your life for the better? Ask yourself another question that could also be transformative.

_____

_____

_____

_____

_____

_____

_____

_____

_____

_____

_____

_____

_____

_____

_____

_____

DAY 99

You must forgive yourself with at least as much regularity as you have been condemning yourself. —ROLF GATES

What can you forgive yourself for?

_____

_____

_____

_____

_____

_____

_____

_____

_____

_____

_____

_____

_____

_____

_____

_____

_____

_____

_____

_____

_____

God is between my thoughts. —UNKNOWN

At this moment, how do you most sense the Divine?

DAY
101

Real transformation begins when you embrace your problems as agents for growth. —MICHAEL A. SINGER

Which of your problems can you embrace as agents for growth and why?

_____

_____

_____

_____

_____

_____

_____

_____

_____

_____

_____

_____

_____

_____

_____

_____

_____

_____

_____

_____

_____

Who you are emotionally often reflects who your parents are. While growing up, it's frequently monkey see, monkey do. For better or worse, you emulate your parents' virtues and faults. If your mother was anxious or a worrywart, chances are she transmitted some of that to you. If your father was a bastion of hope, that came through too. In addition, you may contain interesting dualities of both parents. —JUDITH ORLOFF, MD

How have your parents influenced you emotionally? Is this something you need to recover from, perhaps with help from a professional counselor? If so, make a plan to do so.

_____

_____

_____

_____

_____

_____

_____

_____

_____

_____

_____

_____

_____

_____

_____

DAY 103

The quality of wisdom is more than intellectual, and it is in no way related to how much schooling you have. Exercising wisdom requires cutting through the noise of life and tapping into your core beliefs to make thoughtful decisions. —SUZE ORMAN

What are your core beliefs? Why do you have them and how do you use them to make thoughtful decisions? Do you need to use them more? Why or why not?

_____

_____

_____

_____

_____

_____

_____

_____

_____

_____

_____

_____

_____

_____

_____

_____

When we're looking for compassion, we need someone who is deeply rooted, able to bend, and, most of all, we need someone who embraces us for our strengths and struggles. We need to honor our struggle by sharing it with someone who has earned the right to hear it. When we're looking for compassion, it's about connecting with the right person at the right time about the right issue. —BRENÉ BROWN, PhD

When you need compassion, who do you seek it from? Can you count on them to give it to you? If not, who else might you connect with to meet this need?

_____

_____

_____

_____

_____

_____

_____

_____

_____

_____

_____

_____

_____

_____

_____

_____

DAY 105

The soul's innate essence is wisdom. I also believe we become wise with experience, not age. I know 10-year-olds who are wiser than some 30-year-olds. —ROSIE ACOSTA

From which experiences have you gained the most wisdom and why?

_____

_____

_____

_____

_____

_____

_____

_____

_____

_____

_____

_____

_____

_____

_____

_____

_____

_____

_____

_____

Nothing is as pin-down-able the way we'd like it to be. This is not actually bad news, but we all seem to be programmed for denial. We have absolutely no tolerance for uncertainty. —PEMA CHÖDRÖN

Befriending uncertainty decreases stress in our lives. Identify a significant uncertainty in your life to practice accepting.

_____

_____

_____

_____

_____

_____

_____

_____

_____

_____

_____

_____

_____

_____

_____

_____

_____

DAY 107

To see a World in a Grain of Sand
And a Heaven in a Wild Flower
Hold Infinity in the palm of your hand
And Eternity in an hour . . . —WILLIAM BLAKE

Find a leaf growing on a plant or tree, hold it up to light, preferably sunlight, noting all its intricacies, then journal about connecting to the whole of nature through this activity.

_____

_____

_____

_____

_____

_____

_____

_____

_____

_____

_____

_____

_____

_____

_____

_____

Perception and experience are both created by the mind. The eye and what it sees, the ear and what it hears, the tongue and what it tastes, the nose and what it smells, the nerves and what they feel. —DEEPAK CHOPRA, MD

Among the mind's many capacities is the ability to distort reality in ways that cause unnecessary suffering. To strengthen your ability to perceive with clarity, go outside and use all five senses to note in a nonjudgmental way what you perceive around you. Describe it as if for someone who has never been there and needs to know about it.

DAY 109

I am not a normal man—never have been. The more I accept that, the better I feel. —STEVIE WONDER

What is a difference you have that you would benefit from being more accepting of?

_____

_____

_____

_____

_____

_____

_____

_____

_____

_____

_____

_____

_____

_____

_____

_____

_____

_____

As to what good qualities here may be in our souls, or Who dwells within them, or how precious they are—those are things which we seldom consider and so we trouble little about carefully preserving the soul's beauty. —SAINT TERESA OF AVILA

How do you preserve your soul's beauty?

_____

_____

_____

_____

_____

_____

_____

_____

_____

_____

_____

_____

_____

_____

_____

_____

_____

_____

DAY 111

In this world
Hate never yet dispelled hate.
Only love dispels hate.
This is the law,
Ancient and inexhaustible. —BUDDHA

Journal about a time when you responded to a hateful act with a loving one that helped you sustain your sense of peace. How were you able to do it? How might you use those same skills going forward?

_____

_____

_____

_____

_____

_____

_____

_____

_____

_____

_____

_____

_____

_____

_____

*People don't have time to worry about what you're doing, or how well
you're doing it, because they're all caught up in their own dramas.
People's attention may be drawn to you for a moment (if you succeed or
fail spectacularly and publicly, for instance), but that attention will soon
enough revert right back to where it's always been—on themselves. While it
may seem lonely and horrible at first to imagine that you aren't anyone else's
first order of business, there is also a great release to be found in this idea.
You are free, because everyone is too busy fussing over themselves to worry
all that much about you.* —ELIZABETH GILBERT

Despite how paralyzing self-consciousness can be, it is seldom based on reality.
What tends to make you self-conscious and why? How might you remind yourself
that, in all likelihood, your self-consciousness is based on your illusions instead
of reality?

DAY
113

I became very aware of the existence of spirit when I was a child up on the roof of our garage. I'd lie there in my white flannel nightgown, mesmerized by the night sky, quietly certain that the moon and the stars were my friends. But in addition, I felt that a large force was loving me, something I couldn't name but knew was real. —JUDITH ORLOFF, MD

What is your most memorable spiritual experience?

Instead of unconsciously creating disease, we could be consciously creating health. —DEEPAK CHOPRA, MD

Consistent research proves that people with healthy lifestyles—eating nutritiously, exercising regularly, and not smoking or drinking alcohol excessively—live an average of ten years longer than those who do not. What are you doing to stay physically resilient? If you can improve this, create a plan here to do so.

DAY 115

Individuals have to have the courage and self-respect sufficient to ask,
"Do my social affiliations feed my spirit and enlarge my journey? Or are
they in some way diminishing my journey or asking that I separate from
who I really am?" —JAMES HOLLIS, PhD

What are your most important social affiliations? Do they feed your spirit and
enlarge your journey or diminish you? If so, how might you change this?

_____

_____

_____

_____

_____

_____

_____

_____

_____

_____

_____

_____

_____

_____

_____

_____

_____

_____

*When the compulsive, tyrannical self
sees the inside beauty, it melts.* —SHAMS OF TABRIZ

Look into your heart. What do you see that is beautiful?

_____

_____

_____

_____

_____

_____

_____

_____

_____

_____

_____

_____

_____

_____

_____

_____

_____

_____

The problem in our culture is that when a major thing happens, everyone says, "Pull yourself together," but first you have to give yourself permission to fall apart. It's the natural process. —MARTHA BECK

We all suffer losses—from failed relationships to the deaths of loved ones—and we often feel the need to put up a brave front for others instead of acknowledging the depth of our losses. This can get us stuck in unresolved grief. What is a loss you have experienced that you may benefit from more fully exploring the depth of, perhaps with the guidance of a therapist?

_____

_____

_____

_____

_____

_____

_____

_____

_____

_____

_____

_____

_____

_____

_____

_____

_____

"Hope" is the thing with feathers—
That perches in the soul—
And sings the tune without the words—
And never stops—at all. —EMILY DICKINSON

What has been a source of hope for you lately and why?

_____

_____

_____

_____

_____

_____

_____

_____

_____

_____

_____

_____

_____

_____

_____

_____

_____

_____

_____

DAY
119

Each of us must face a moment in our lives called "the breakdown moment."
This is the time when you must stand toe to toe, eyeball to eyeball, with the
very thing you have tried desperately to avoid. —IYANLA VANZANT

What was a "breakdown moment" for you and what did it teach you?

_____

_____

_____

_____

_____

_____

_____

_____

_____

_____

_____

_____

_____

_____

_____

_____

_____

_____

Practice, or abhyasa, *is the will to repeatedly align and realign attention to the present moment, the only place where the singular process of yoking consciousness into profound stillness can be enacted. Sustained effort is required because the forces of distraction are strong and unrelenting.* —CHIP HARTRANFT

Candle gazing is a way many people have found to be effective for stilling the mind and reconnecting to the present moment. Light a candle and gaze at its flame for at least five minutes, perhaps while listening to soft, relaxing music, then journal about the effect of this.

_____

_____

_____

_____

_____

_____

_____

_____

_____

_____

_____

_____

_____

_____

_____

You have been told that, even like a chain, you are as weak as your weakest link. This is but half the truth. You are also as strong as your strongest link. —KHALIL GIBRAN

What are your most significant strengths and how do you use them? Are there ways to use them more? If so, create a plan to do so here.

_____

_____

_____

_____

_____

_____

_____

_____

_____

_____

_____

_____

_____

_____

_____

_____

_____

_____

I devote my day to blessing those whom I do not like, knowing that if I knew them as God knows them, then I would love them as He does. I ask not that they change but that I might see them more clearly. May their innocence become obvious to me. —MARIANNE WILLIAMSON

Picture in your mind someone whom you very much dislike. Take a few mindful breaths and do your best to picture them from the viewpoint of a loving spiritual entity, then write about this experience.

_____

_____

_____

_____

_____

_____

_____

_____

_____

_____

_____

_____

_____

_____

_____

_____

My only escape from a troublesome family life was reading. —ISABEL ALLENDE

What was your escape from challenging interactions with family, especially when you were growing up? Is it still an escape for you? Why or why not?

_____

_____

_____

_____

_____

_____

_____

_____

_____

_____

_____

_____

_____

_____

_____

_____

_____

_____

_____

I do hope that people can relate and understand that it's O.K. to not be O.K., and it's O.K. to talk about it. There are people who can help, and there is usually a light at the end of any tunnel. —NAOMI OSAKA

Who helps you when it is hard to cope? Who else might you reach out to?

_____

_____

_____

_____

_____

_____

_____

_____

_____

_____

_____

_____

_____

_____

_____

_____

DAY
125

The fullness of joy is to behold God in everything. —JULIAN OF NORWICH

In whom and what do you most see God and why?

_____

_____

_____

_____

_____

_____

_____

_____

_____

_____

_____

_____

_____

_____

_____

_____

My most formidable opponent is a man named Mohandas K. Gandhi.
—MOHANDAS K. GANDHI

In what ways are you your most formidable opponent? How might you change this?

_____

_____

_____

_____

_____

_____

_____

_____

_____

_____

_____

_____

_____

_____

_____

_____

_____

DAY
127

But while much is important, very little is urgent. Understanding this is the threshold to peace. For while surviving demands a great deal from us to get from day to day, being alive asks nothing of us. Stripped of our urgency, being alive is its own reward. —MARK NEPO

What are things you tend to believe are urgent that really are not? Simply journaling about them can help reduce the pressure you put on yourself about them.

_____

_____

_____

_____

_____

_____

_____

_____

_____

_____

_____

_____

_____

_____

_____

_____

What we often don't realize is that whatever dynamics we learned from our first families tend to be mirrored in the way we treat ourselves. —JULIE PETERSON

How do you treat yourself based upon how your family of origin treated you? If this is something you need to change, develop a plan to do so.

_____

_____

_____

_____

_____

_____

_____

_____

_____

_____

_____

_____

_____

_____

_____

_____

_____

_____

DAY 129

Compassion allows me to see the points of view of those whom I am not in agreement with in order to learn something about myself and the ways I respond to—and at times lack compassion for—myself. It looks like being still, allowing myself to be held, and allowing the tears to flow. —CHELSEA JACKSON ROBERTS

Journal about a time when showing compassion to someone you disagreed with helped you learn something important about yourself.

_____

_____

_____

_____

_____

_____

_____

_____

_____

_____

_____

_____

_____

_____

_____

_____

_____

From the Buddhist viewpoint, every event has many aspects, and naturally,
one event can be viewed from many, many different angles. It is very rare
or almost impossible that an event can be negative from all points of view.
Therefore, it is useful when something happens to try to look at it from
different angles. —DALAI LAMA XIV

Use the space below to write about a difficult issue from a fresh point of view.

We return to the mountains
For strength
To know that the edge of one peak
Flies our sight out
To the farthest one where beyond
All things there is a heaven
Within us
Teaching us our wings. —LAURA HOPE-GILL

What are sources of emotional strength for you and why? Do you need more? If so, how might you connect with them?

_____

_____

_____

_____

_____

_____

_____

_____

_____

_____

_____

_____

_____

If someone can prove me wrong and show me my mistakes in any thought or action, I shall gladly change. I seek the truth, which never harmed anyone: the harm is to persist in one's own self-deception and ignorance. —MARCUS AURELIUS

Accepting criticism, even the most valid, can be challenging, but it is a powerful way to recognize our mistakes, correct them, and learn from them, which helps us become more resilient. Write about a time when you were able to do this.

_____

_____

_____

_____

_____

_____

_____

_____

_____

_____

_____

_____

_____

_____

_____

_____

DAY
133

Habitually contemplate whether your thoughts stem from love or from fear. If your thoughts originate in love, then follow them. But if they originate from a place of fear, then dig deep to find the root of your fear. —TIMBER HAWKEYE

What are your biggest fears? Are they based on reality or distortions of it? How can you constructively address them?

_____

_____

_____

_____

_____

_____

_____

_____

_____

_____

_____

_____

_____

_____

_____

_____

_____

A human being is part of the whole, called by us the "universe," a part limited in time and space. He experiences himself, his thoughts and feelings, as something separate from the rest—a kind of optical delusion of his consciousness. This delusion is a kind of prison for us, restricting us to our personal desires and to affection for a few persons nearest to us. Our task must be to free ourselves from this prison by widening our circle of compassion to embrace all living creatures and the whole nature in its beauty. —ALBERT EINSTEIN

Widening our circle of compassion. At first glance, it can seem like an intimidating goal, but it can be as simple as planting flowers for others to see.

What are ways you can widen your circle of compassion? Identify a target date you will follow through with this.

_____

_____

_____

_____

_____

_____

_____

_____

_____

_____

_____

_____

_____

_____

Problems are messages. —SHAKTI GAWAIN

What are your most significant problems telling you?

_____

_____

_____

_____

_____

_____

_____

_____

_____

_____

_____

_____

_____

_____

_____

_____

_____

_____

_____

_____

_____

Are you considering becoming a creative person? Too late, you already are one. To call somebody "a creative person" is almost laughably redundant; creativity is the hallmark of our species. —ELIZABETH GILBERT

What are some of the most creative things you have ever done and what inspired you to do them?

_____

_____

_____

_____

_____

_____

_____

_____

_____

_____

_____

_____

_____

_____

_____

_____

DAY 137

Time is our most precious resource, but very few of us use it as wisely as we should. We rush through our lives with our eyes on our phones, trying to get through one thing after another. We rush around trying to get somewhere that we think will make us happy. We rush around so much that in the midst of it all, we forget to actually live.

Do you make time to live? Time for yourself? Time for your friends? Time for your family? Or are you too busy? —MARIA SHRIVER

What are your answers to these questions?

_____

_____

_____

_____

_____

_____

_____

_____

_____

_____

_____

_____

_____

_____

_____

_____

_____

_____

They can be like the sun, words. They can do for the heart what light can do for a field. —SAINT JOHN OF THE CROSS

Recount a time when someone said something to you that lifted you up and a time when you did the same for someone else.

_____

_____

_____

_____

_____

_____

_____

_____

_____

_____

_____

_____

_____

_____

_____

_____

_____

When you practice walking meditation and release some of your sorrow and your anger, when you look deeply into things and shed some of your misperceptions, cravings, and attachments, you discover the body of the Dharma, the body of bliss, and the body of transformation within you. —THICH NHAT HANH

Whether indoors or outside, walk for about ten minutes, and with each step, repeat a word or short phrase that helps soothe you, then journal about the experience.

_____

_____

_____

_____

_____

_____

_____

_____

_____

_____

_____

_____

_____

_____

_____

_____

_____

I've been teaching [yoga] for over 25 years, and I can tell you that when people feel stiff or have a little tweak somewhere, the negative self-talk starts. Then there's usually some withdrawal from self-care. —SHIVA REA

Instead of withdrawing from self-care when we have physical discomforts, we can use them as impetuses to nurture ourselves. So take a few minutes to gently massage any place on your body that feels stiff or sore or simply could benefit from your loving touch. Do this while breathing mindfully and perhaps listening to soft, calming music, then journal about how it felt.

_____

_____

_____

_____

_____

_____

_____

_____

_____

_____

_____

_____

_____

DAY
141

You need to remember that we are all created creative and can invent new scenarios as frequently as they are needed. —MAYA ANGELOU

Journal about a time that you used your creativity to successfully adapt to an upsetting change. How might you use those same skills now?

_____

_____

_____

_____

_____

_____

_____

_____

_____

_____

_____

_____

_____

_____

_____

_____

_____

_____

_____

_____

The great salt marsh spreading all around as far as my eye could see has remained the central image that runs throughout my work. I cannot look at a salt marsh, veined with salt creeks swollen with the moonstruck tides, without believing in God. —PAT CONROY

Where do you see the Divine and why?

DAY
143

Growth is a tangled spiral, not a straight line. Try not to put a time limit on it. You may need to have the same realization 1,000 times over the course of transformation. Most long-standing patterns didn't develop in a day, and they won't change in a day, either. —SHIVANI HAWKINS

Write about an important realization you frequently need to remind yourself of.

Committing to a life of purpose takes courage. There was a time in my own life when I felt torn between who the world was telling me I should be and what I felt to be the truth of myself. Today, I know for sure what I'm here to do. That's because I started listening to my instincts and paying attention to the decisions I made each and every day. —OPRAH WINFREY

What are you here on earth to do? Where are you in your journey in accomplishing this? What else do you need to do to fulfill this purpose?

_____

_____

_____

_____

_____

_____

_____

_____

_____

_____

_____

_____

_____

_____

_____

_____

_____

DAY
145

Each one should test their own actions. Then they can take pride in themselves alone, without comparing themselves to someone else. —GALATIANS 6:4

The pervasive habit of comparing ourselves with others tends to give us a false sense of inferiority or superiority, both of which impair our ability to meaningfully connect with others. Recount a time when you compared yourself with others and what you learned from it that can help you now.

_____

_____

_____

_____

_____

_____

_____

_____

_____

_____

_____

_____

_____

_____

_____

_____

_____

I have fibromyalgia, and although living with chronic physical pain is difficult, I've radically accepted that while I cannot think my way out of this problem, I can behave my way out of it with distress tolerance skills and routines. —LADY GAGA

What is a pain—either physical or mental—that you would benefit from practicing radical acceptance of, acknowledging it without letting it control your life?

_____

_____

_____

_____

_____

_____

_____

_____

_____

_____

_____

_____

_____

_____

_____

_____

_____

A veteran myself of three breakdowns, I have had to learn to live each day very carefully. I must write. I must walk. I must pray. I must content myself with small amounts of progress. Above all, I must not binge on drama and despair. —JULIA CAMERON

Surviving traumatic events can show us what we need to do for our well-being. What are they for you? Do you do them on a regular basis? If not, detail a plan to do so.

Sometimes I think people just want to stay on the quick-fix path of searching for the "esoteric alchemy" to magically blossom their life into the life they think they want. That alchemy exists, but it requires us to live a spiritual life. —PAUL SUTHERLAND

What has been the quality of your spiritual life lately? How can you improve it?

_____

_____

_____

_____

_____

_____

_____

_____

_____

_____

_____

_____

_____

_____

_____

_____

_____

_____

DAY
149

A great teacher or mentor allows you to discover something for yourself—which is different from telling you the answer—and does not rush the process. I have been so fortunate in my life to have had many masterful teachers and mentors. They have all inspired me to be a better version of myself in various ways. —BARON BAPTISTE

Who have been great teachers or mentors for you and how have they helped you to grow?

_____

_____

_____

_____

_____

_____

_____

_____

_____

_____

_____

_____

_____

_____

_____

_____

_____

_____

I find that the most creative time I have is when I do meditation—sitting or walking. I'm not trying to resolve a dilemma or figure something out. It's just that in the process of meditating, a greater spaciousness is created in my mind, and that's when the creative solution or next step for something appears naturally. —SHARON SALZBERG

Our best solutions and ideas often come to us when we are engaged in something meditatively—anything from sitting quietly to slicing vegetables. Describe a time when this occurred for you.

_____

_____

_____

_____

_____

_____

_____

_____

_____

_____

_____

_____

_____

_____

_____

_____

Anything you say from your heart to God is a prayer. —ANNE LAMOTT

Take a few mindful breaths, then use the space below to write a prayer.

_____

_____

_____

_____

_____

_____

_____

_____

_____

_____

_____

_____

_____

_____

_____

_____

_____

_____

_____

The data suggest that social connections extend our life span, help us fight off disease, even make us enjoy what we eat more. Yet when you tell people to talk to strangers, they think This is gonna be horrible. *But people are excited that you want to relate to them. By and large, the practice makes us feel better.* —LAURIE SANTOS, PHD

Recount a time that you struck up an enjoyable conversation with a stranger. How might you do that more often?

_____

_____

_____

_____

_____

_____

_____

_____

_____

_____

_____

_____

_____

_____

_____

_____

*I know a cure for sadness: Let your hands
touch something that makes your eyes
smile.* —MIRABAI

Identify and touch—indeed, caress—something that brings you joy, then write
about it.

_____

_____

_____

_____

_____

_____

_____

_____

_____

_____

_____

_____

_____

_____

_____

_____

_____

Someone who is truly awakened practices mindfulness not only while in meditation, paying attention to the breath, but when engaged in daily routine activities. —VICTOR M. PARACHIN, MDiv

Do a routine activity as if for the very first time, noting everything about it, including why you are doing it, then journal about the experience.

Dreaming, after all, is a form of planning. —GLORIA STEINEM

Which of your dreams has been most inspirational and why?

_____

_____

_____

_____

_____

_____

_____

_____

_____

_____

_____

_____

_____

_____

_____

_____

_____

_____

_____

One way to engage or reengage with passion in your life is to identify where you lose it, where it drains out. Maybe it's a job that sucks the life out of you or a relationship where you feel like a ghost of your full self. —GREGG LEVOY

What tends to drain your passion in life and what can you do about it?

_____

_____

_____

_____

_____

_____

_____

_____

_____

_____

_____

_____

_____

_____

_____

_____

_____

_____

_____

I paid the price of time
Of sacrifice
Of limb
I paid the price to share with you Beauty and Truth
The veil, you see, is thin
I linger and wait
Above and within
To bring my splendor, power, and truth. —KATHRYN MORSE MORGANELLI

Whom have you recently shared Beauty and Truth with and how did you do it?

_____

_____

_____

_____

_____

_____

_____

_____

_____

_____

_____

_____

_____

_____

_____

_____

When my husband died more than 20 years ago, I remember wondering, How will I get through the rest of my life? I decided not to think about that, but to just have a cup of coffee. The coffee tasted good. It was a nice day. Bit by bit, the years went by. —ANNE TYLER

Which loss did you think you could not survive but did? How did you do it? What continues to resonate about this emotional journey?

_____

_____

_____

_____

_____

_____

_____

_____

_____

_____

_____

_____

_____

_____

_____

_____

DAY 159

It is easy to find reasons not to be responsible. In fact, many of us are not aware of how we do it or that we do it at all. Not taking responsibility for your life means blaming, finding causes, excuses and reasons for what is going on in your life as if they had nothing to do with you. —IYANLA VANZANT

Why do we so often like to blame others for issues in our lives? Because it is easier than taking responsibility for them, and yet that is the first step to solving them. What is an issue that you tend to blame others for that you would benefit from taking responsibility for?

_____

_____

_____

_____

_____

_____

_____

_____

_____

_____

_____

_____

_____

_____

_____

_____

Poetry is the tool that I use to see myself more clearly. —JACQUELINE SUSKIN

What helps you see yourself more clearly? Do you use it often enough? If not, make a plan to do so.

_____

_____

_____

_____

_____

_____

_____

_____

_____

_____

_____

_____

_____

_____

_____

_____

DAY
161

Shame hates it when we reach out and tell our story. It hates having words wrapped around it—it can't survive being shared. —BRENÉ BROWN, PhD

We have all done things we are not proud of, but instead of allowing shame to imprison us, we can free ourselves from it by opening up to a trustworthy family member, close friend, or counselor. Do you have someone with whom you can share your most shameful secrets? If so, who? If not, who might you reach out to?

Great emergencies and crises show us how much greater our vital resources are than we had supposed. —WILLIAM JAMES

Write about a great emergency or crisis in which you discovered important resources you did not realize you had. What did this teach you?

_____

_____

_____

_____

_____

_____

_____

_____

_____

_____

_____

_____

_____

_____

_____

_____

DAY
163

Optimism shouldn't be seen as opposed to pessimism, but in conversation with it. Your optimism will never be as powerful as it is in that exact moment when you want to give it up. —AMANDA GORMAN

Recall a time when you tenaciously remained optimistic despite being in a difficult situation. What helped you remain optimistic? How might it help you with current challenges?

_____

_____

_____

_____

_____

_____

_____

_____

_____

_____

_____

_____

_____

_____

_____

_____

_____

Be your own master, and look at things as a man, as a human being, as a
citizen, as a mortal creature. And here are two of the most immediately
useful thoughts you will dip into. First, that things cannot touch the mind:
they are external and inert; anxieties can only come from your internal
judgment. Second, that all these things you see will change almost as you
look at them, and then will be no more. —MARCUS AURELIUS

Our internal judgments often distort things into problems that cause unnecessary
turmoil. Strengthening the ability to correct initial misperceptions often makes
"problems" disappear along with the related stress. Recount a time when you
were able to do that and what you learned from the situation.

_____

_____

_____

_____

_____

_____

_____

_____

_____

_____

_____

_____

_____

_____

DAY 165

It is God's will that we take His behests and His comfortings as largely and as mightily as we may take them, and also He willeth that we take our abiding and our troubles as lightly as we may take them, and set them at nought. For the more lightly we take them, and the less price we set on them, for love, the less pain we shall have in the feeling of them.... —JULIAN OF NORWICH

It is easy to give our problems more significance in our lives than they deserve. Which might be some for you?

_____

_____

_____

_____

_____

_____

_____

_____

_____

_____

_____

_____

_____

_____

_____

_____

_____

The deepest reality you are aware of is the one from which you draw your power. —DEEPAK CHOPRA, MD

What is your deepest reality that you are most aware of and from which you draw power?

_____

_____

_____

_____

_____

_____

_____

_____

_____

_____

_____

_____

_____

_____

_____

_____

You already have the gold coins beneath you, of presence, creativity, intimacy, time for wonder, and nature, and life. Oh, yeah, you say? And where would those rascally coins be?

This is what I say: First of all, no one needs to watch the news every night, unless one is married to the anchor. —ANNE LAMOTT

What regular activity can you spend less time on to create more time for true presence, creativity, intimacy, wonder, nature, and life itself?

_____

_____

_____

_____

_____

_____

_____

_____

_____

_____

_____

_____

_____

_____

If you can sit with the pain or discomfort, you may discover the deeper truth behind what you are experiencing. In the presence of this truth, the mind chatter stops and it becomes easier to hear the voice of a deeper wisdom. —SHIVANI HAWKINS

Take a few minutes to breathe mindfully, then write whatever your deeper wisdom is telling you at this moment.

_____

_____

_____

_____

_____

_____

_____

_____

_____

_____

_____

_____

_____

_____

_____

We are continually exposed to the toxins of stress, speed, pressure, and negative thoughts and emotions both from ourselves and others. These things are often more powerful and destructive than the environmental toxins we worry about. —THOMAS BIEN, PHD, AND BEVERLY BIEN, MEd

How do you typically respond to stress and how effective is it? If it is not as effective as you need it to be, what alternatives can you try?

_____

_____

_____

_____

_____

_____

_____

_____

_____

_____

_____

_____

_____

_____

_____

_____

It can often feel like our bodies are working against us. They aren't! Our bodies are always trying to help us, always trying to communicate what they need. They don't always do it very well or conveniently, but when we get better at listening we can help ourselves return to balance. —JULIE PETERS

Take a few minutes to listen to your body. What is it telling you that it needs?

_____

_____

_____

_____

_____

_____

_____

_____

_____

_____

_____

_____

_____

_____

_____

_____

_____

DAY
171

Each of us has lived through some devastation, some loneliness, some weather superstorm or spiritual superstorm, when we look at each other we must say, I understand. I understand how you feel because I have been there myself. —MAYA ANGELOU

Journal about a time when you connected with someone who experienced a similar hardship to yours. How were you able to support each other?

_____

_____

_____

_____

_____

_____

_____

_____

_____

_____

_____

_____

_____

_____

_____

_____

_____

*Minding other people's business simply isn't the work we are here to do,
regardless of how seductive the idea may be. We must make our own journey,
and even when it appears that someone we love is making a poor decision
about an important matter, unless we are asked for advice, it's not our place
to offer it.* —KAREN CASEY, PhD

Recall a time when you received unasked-for advice and when you gave it. What
did you learn from these experiences?

DAY 173

Depression and anxiety are a real thing and there are a lot of people who struggle to get out of it. Feeling a way to express what is inside of you is key. I can't always express it perfectly for myself, but I hear it and I feel it in a song. Then something in me cracks open, tears start to flow, and I feel restored. —MICHAEL FRANTI

How do you deal with depression and anxiety? What may be other ways to try?

_____

_____

_____

_____

_____

_____

_____

_____

_____

_____

_____

_____

_____

_____

_____

_____

_____

_____

*We each exist on our own planet with its own rules, assumptions, and
conclusions, most of which we created so long ago that we're not even
consciously aware of them. We're not seeing life as it is, but as we
conclude it to be.*

*This can be very dangerous, particularly in times of change, when being
in touch with current reality is very important. How can you ride the wave
of change if you don't even have an accurate picture of what direction it's
coming from or at what speed?* —M. J. RYAN

Recount a time when you reacted to a change based on assumptions about it
instead of reality, and then a time when you reacted to change based on reality,
even if that reality was unpleasant. What were the results of both experiences and
what did you learn from them?

_____

_____

_____

_____

_____

_____

_____

_____

_____

_____

_____

_____

_____

DAY
175

With its flat dusty landscape as far as the eye can see, the great blue ceiling above, the endless stretches of yellow mealie fields, scrub and bushes, the Free State's landscape gladdens my heart no matter what my mood. When I am there I feel like nothing can shut me in, that my thoughts can roam as far and wide as the horizons. —NELSON MANDELA

Which place most helps you to free your mind? How can you spend more time there?

_____

_____

_____

_____

_____

_____

_____

_____

_____

_____

_____

_____

_____

_____

_____

_____

_____

The one who seeks
the spiritual path
is sought after by the spirit. —HAZRAT INAYAT KHAN

What kind of spiritual path are you seeking or are on now and why?

_____

_____

_____

_____

_____

_____

_____

_____

_____

_____

_____

_____

_____

_____

_____

_____

_____

DAY 177

As I have found in my own life, it is often not until crisis that we are able to crack open our protective shells and attend to our deepest wounds. —JOSEFA RANGEL, MD

What are your deepest wounds? How are you addressing them? Is what you are doing effective or would you benefit by doing more, such as getting professional counseling?

_____

_____

_____

_____

_____

_____

_____

_____

_____

_____

_____

_____

_____

_____

_____

In meditation, the mind wanders from its anchor every few breaths, providing us with numerous opportunities to acknowledge, accept, and eventually learn from things not going our way. —ROLF GATES

Get into a comfortable position and place a hand at the center of your chest. While taking slow, steady breaths, watch your hand move outward with each inhalation, and inward with each exhalation. Repeat this for five to ten minutes, then journal about how you feel.

DAY
179

Long before you were conceived by your parents, you were conceived in the mind of God. He thought of you first. It is not fate, nor chance, nor luck, nor coincidence that you are breathing at this very moment. —RICK WARREN

Use the space below to pour out your heart and soul to the God of your understanding.

_____

_____

_____

_____

_____

_____

_____

_____

_____

_____

_____

_____

_____

_____

_____

_____

_____

_____

Only you can take inner freedom away from yourself, or give it to yourself.
Nobody else can. It doesn't matter what others do, unless you decide that
it matters to you. Begin with small things. We tend to let ourselves get
bothered by the little, meaningless things that happen every day.
—MICHAEL A. SINGER

Identify a few small, meaningless things that sometimes occur that you can
practice observing in a neutral way instead of being bothered by them.

_____

_____

_____

_____

_____

_____

_____

_____

_____

_____

_____

_____

_____

_____

_____

_____

_____

DAY
181

It is what you do for others that will last. —CARMELO ANTHONY

What significant things are you doing for others?

_____

_____

_____

_____

_____

_____

_____

_____

_____

_____

_____

_____

_____

_____

_____

_____

_____

_____

_____

_____

Troubled?
Then stay with me,
for I'm not. —HAFIZ

DAY
182

Is there anyone in your life who is a source of calm for you during the storms of life? If so, who is it and how do they calm you? If you do not have anyone to meet this need, how might you change this?

_____

_____

_____

_____

_____

_____

_____

_____

_____

_____

_____

_____

_____

_____

_____

_____

_____

DAY 183

Not-knowing is true knowledge.
Presuming to know is a disease.
First realize that you are sick;
Then you can move toward health. —LAO TZU

What is a presumption you would benefit from letting go of?

_____

_____

_____

_____

_____

_____

_____

_____

_____

_____

_____

_____

_____

_____

_____

_____

_____

_____

God meets us more than halfway if we undertake the simplest of motions toward Him. —JULIA CAMERON

What motions are you making toward the Divine?

_____

_____

_____

_____

_____

_____

_____

_____

_____

_____

_____

_____

_____

_____

_____

_____

_____

_____

As a kid I understood that people were different colors, but in my head white and black and brown were like types of chocolate. Dad was the white chocolate, Mom was the dark chocolate, and I was the milk chocolate. But we were all just chocolate. —TREVOR NOAH

According to the U.S. National Institutes of Health, all human beings are 99.9 percent identical in their genetic makeup. It is only 0.1 percent that makes us different colors and yet we can often allow that tiny percentage to separate us from others. How many of the people close to you are of a different race than you? How might you create more diversity in your relationships?

_____

_____

_____

_____

_____

_____

_____

_____

_____

_____

_____

_____

_____

_____

_____

_____

See if you can catch yourself complaining, in either speech or thought, about a situation you find yourself in, what other people do or say, your surroundings, your life situation, even the weather. To complain is always nonacceptance of what is. It invariably carries an unconscious negative charge. When you complain, you make yourself into a victim. When you speak out, you are in your power. —ECKHART TOLLE

What do you tend to complain about? What are more constructive options?

_____

_____

_____

_____

_____

_____

_____

_____

_____

_____

_____

_____

_____

_____

_____

_____

No expansion or evolution can take place without change, and periods of change are not always comfortable. —MICHAEL A. SINGER

What was a major change that was uncomfortable, but which you emerged better for?

_____

_____

_____

_____

_____

_____

_____

_____

_____

_____

_____

_____

_____

_____

_____

_____

*Being present is easier said than done, of course. Presence requires letting
go of old habits, complaints, and hang-ups. In my case, it also required
recognizing my competitiveness and impatience; I had to step back to notice
the ways I am hard on people, judging them when I should just support them,
insisting things be done on my punishing schedule. Today I make more time
to sit and listen when a friend is troubled by something. I climb fewer hills.*
—MARGARET O'ROURKE

What impacts your ability to be truly present with the people who mean the most
to you and what can you do about it?

DAY
189

Here's an idea: How's about you spend less time on relationships in which you feel like Charlie Brown, trying to kick the ball Lucy invariably pulls away, and spend more time with people who don't leave you crushed and disappointed over and over again? Go for the people who are waiting to love you. Because they do exist. —MARTHA BECK

Are there people in your life who are toxic for you? If so, who are they? Use the space below to commit to withdrawing from them and seeking others who will support you.

_____

_____

_____

_____

_____

_____

_____

_____

_____

_____

_____

_____

_____

_____

Addiction doesn't have to be to drugs, alcohol, or cigarettes. Addiction is what I do reflexively to lower the distress I'm feeling—whether I'm aware of my doing it or not. —JAMES HOLLIS, PhD

What is your default way of reducing stress? How constructive is it? If it is not as helpful as you need it to be, what are better alternatives?

_____

_____

_____

_____

_____

_____

_____

_____

_____

_____

_____

_____

_____

_____

_____

_____

_____

_____

_____

Life is all about making choices and I'm very happy with mine. —MERYL STREEP

How happy are you with the major choices you have made? If you are unhappy with them, what can you do about it?

_____

_____

_____

_____

_____

_____

_____

_____

_____

_____

_____

_____

_____

_____

_____

_____

_____

_____

_____

If you want to enjoy your power in your life, you must have a plan for your physical body. More important, you must follow the plan. —IYANLA VANZANT

Do you have a plan for taking care of yourself physically? If so, what is it? More important, are you following it? What would help you increase your adherence to it?

_____

_____

_____

_____

_____

_____

_____

_____

_____

_____

_____

_____

_____

_____

_____

_____

_____

Healing includes letting our ongoing experience of being a wounded human being deepen our compassion for others. —KEVIN ANDERSON, PhD

What is a wounding experience that you went through that has deepened your compassion for others and why?

_____

_____

_____

_____

_____

_____

_____

_____

_____

_____

_____

_____

_____

_____

_____

_____

_____

I have long said that self-worth determines one's net worth. When you are silent, or silenced, it's very hard to get in touch with your self-worth. It is only when you speak your truth that you can be truly powerful.
—SUZE ORMAN

Detail an important time when you spoke your truth even though others did not want to hear it. What most resonates from this experience?

_____

_____

_____

_____

_____

_____

_____

_____

_____

_____

_____

_____

_____

_____

_____

_____

My game plan was to keep working at Red Lobster, get my truck driver's license and kind of drive a truck like my dad . . . if you would have offered me in, like 1989, '90, right before I got on Saturday Night Live, *if you would have offered me a job that paid $10, $12 an hour, I would have never told another joke in my life.* —CHRIS ROCK

Had Chris Rock gotten what he wanted when he was a teenager, he never would have become one of the world's most famous—and thought-provoking—comedians. Journal about a time when an unexpected opportunity positively altered your plans.

_____

_____

_____

_____

_____

_____

_____

_____

_____

_____

_____

_____

_____

_____

_____

_____

_____

*One of the most damaging ideas our culture perpetuates is the idea that
we cannot trust ourselves or our perceptions. We are raised to doubt
ourselves, to seek outside validation for our perceptions, to assume that
someone other than ourselves can tell us our truth more clearly than we
can tell ourselves.* —JULIA CAMERON

Recount a time when you trusted yourself about a major issue and a time when
you did not. What were the results of these circumstances and what did you learn
from them?

_____

_____

_____

_____

_____

_____

_____

_____

_____

_____

_____

_____

_____

_____

_____

_____

DAY
197

The mind is a superb instrument if used rightly. Used wrongly, however, it becomes very destructive. To put it more accurately, it is not so much that you use your mind wrongly—you usually don't use it at all. It uses you. This is the disease. You believe that you are your mind. This is the delusion. The instrument has taken you over. —ECKHART TOLLE

You are not your mind. You are not the thoughts your mind produces. You are the larger witness of them and, with practice, you will see that most of your thoughts have no more substance than words written on the surface of water.

As part of this practice, fill a sink or tub with water, write your thoughts upon the surface of it, and witness them disappear in the water just like they can from your mind.

_____

_____

_____

_____

_____

_____

_____

_____

_____

_____

_____

_____

_____

"Yes" is the only password we need as we face the struggles on our journey through life. It is another way of saying, "Thy will be done" because it is a yes to what we cannot change, only bow to. —DAVID RICHO, PhD

What is something that you have no control over that you can practice saying "yes" to instead of "no" to to create more peace and balance in your life?

_____

_____

_____

_____

_____

_____

_____

_____

_____

_____

_____

_____

_____

_____

_____

_____

_____

The power of place is that it connects us to our pasts and, often, to our dreams of the future. —NATASHA TRETHEWEY

What place connects you to your dreams for your future? Are you already living in this place? If not, how can you lay the groundwork for getting there?

_____

_____

_____

_____

_____

_____

_____

_____

_____

_____

_____

_____

_____

_____

_____

_____

_____

_____

We're drenched in a 24-hour news cycle that is curated to make us feel afraid—so we watch more news. —JULIE PETERS

How much time do you normally spend watching or reading the news? How does it affect you?

_____

_____

_____

_____

_____

_____

_____

_____

_____

_____

_____

_____

_____

_____

_____

_____

_____

_____

_____

I take self-love very seriously because when I was younger, I wanted to change everything about myself. I didn't love who I was. —LIZZO

Do you love who you are? If so, why? If not, how might you change this?

_____

_____

_____

_____

_____

_____

_____

_____

_____

_____

_____

_____

_____

_____

_____

_____

_____

_____

Nature's beauty speaks to me and expands my sense of self. My being. My soul. —OPRAH WINFREY

Go outside or look out the window. Note everything you sense in the natural world that transports you.

_____

_____

_____

_____

_____

_____

_____

_____

_____

_____

_____

_____

_____

_____

_____

_____

_____

_____

DAY 203

I don't think I've ever been fearless. Instead, I'm afraid and I do it anyway. —JENNIFER PASTILOFF

Recount a time when you completed a major accomplishment despite fear.

_____

_____

_____

_____

_____

_____

_____

_____

_____

_____

_____

_____

_____

_____

_____

_____

_____

_____

I need calm and quiet if I am to work, but I need a certain amount of stimulation, too. It's really a juggling act. I must be a gatekeeper on the traffic in my life. Too much traffic and I grow overwhelmed. Too little and I grow stagnant. It's a balance that I am seeking and I must be attentive because my needs are always shifting. —JULIA CAMERON

How effective are you in being the gatekeeper of the traffic in your life? If you need to, how can you improve the balance between quiet and stimulation?

Recently, a friend asked me if I'd ever been to Israel. Before I could even open my mouth, she added slyly, "Oh, that's right. You can't get on a plane." I think she was trying to be funny.

There was a time when I would have died a thousand deaths: She knows my dirty secret; she's making fun of me; she thinks I'm pathetic; I am, in fact, pathetic. *This time, however, I stopped the tape in my head and played a new one. It said,* Everyone has a screw loose somewhere, and having a thing about planes happens to be mine. —BETH LEVINE

We all have negative tapes in our heads that we can allow various people and things to trigger. What are some for you and how can you reframe them in a self-affirming way?

_____

_____

_____

_____

_____

_____

_____

_____

_____

_____

_____

_____

_____

If you never test your limits, you'll never know what they are.
—NICOLE CALHOUN, PhD

Journal about the most recent time that you tested your limits and what you learned from doing so.

_____

_____

_____

_____

_____

_____

_____

_____

_____

_____

_____

_____

_____

_____

_____

_____

_____

_____

DAY 207

Something so hard can be so easy if you just have a little help. In the right place, under the right conditions, you can finally stretch into what you're supposed to be. —HOPE JAHREN, PhD

While it can be hard to ask for help, there are times when we need it to stretch into who we are supposed to be. Is there an important aspect of your life that you need help with? If so, what is it and who might help you with it?

_____

_____

_____

_____

_____

_____

_____

_____

_____

_____

_____

_____

_____

_____

_____

_____

_____

_____

I'm everything and nothing at all. I'm black, I'm white, I'm male, female. To me, seeing all the facets of yourself is the next level of our evolution— understanding who we really are. —RuPAUL

What are the most important facets of yourself and why?

_____

_____

_____

_____

_____

_____

_____

_____

_____

_____

_____

_____

_____

_____

_____

_____

_____

DAY
209

Dear wayfarer, now indulge me in a sober moment.
Please set down your glass.
I can help you write a letter of resignation
to all your fears and sadness. —HAFIZ

Use the space below to write a letter of resignation to your most significant sources of fear and sadness.

_____

_____

_____

_____

_____

_____

_____

_____

_____

_____

_____

_____

_____

_____

_____

_____

Illness can be an invitation to explore the wholeness of our lives and tend to all areas of disharmony with self-love and care. When health challenges arise, in addition to seeking helpful medical care, we can remember to return to ourselves. —JOSEFA RANGEL, MD

Physical illnesses can be important teachers—if we allow them to be. For example, they can be signs that we need to slow down and take better care of ourselves. What lessons have you learned from experiencing illnesses?

_____

_____

_____

_____

_____

_____

_____

_____

_____

_____

_____

_____

_____

_____

_____

_____

_____

To attain true inner freedom, you must be able to objectively watch your problems instead of being lost in them. No solution can possibly exist while you're lost in the energy of a problem. —MICHAEL A. SINGER

Which problem do you often get lost in and why? Journaling about it can be the first step toward being able to see it more clearly.

I've tried to tease out the alchemy that makes wild swimming so vital to my mental health. Perhaps it is the physicality of plunging myself into water, the cold so absolute it is all I am, taking me out of my mind and into my body so I become a heart beating fast to pump blood, muscles working to keep warm, on fire in the best way. —KIRAN MILLWOOD HARGRAVE

What is vital to your mental health and why? How might you integrate more of it in your life to help you become more resilient?

_____

_____

_____

_____

_____

_____

_____

_____

_____

_____

_____

_____

_____

_____

_____

_____

At the center of every problem, the answer is present. —IYANLA VANZANT

What was the most recent major problem you solved and what did you learn from doing so that you can continue to apply in your life?

_____

_____

_____

_____

_____

_____

_____

_____

_____

_____

_____

_____

_____

_____

_____

_____

_____

_____

What causes fights and quarrels among you? Don't they come from your desires that battle within you? —JAMES 4:1

What are your frequent inner conflicts and how might you free yourself from them?

_____

_____

_____

_____

_____

_____

_____

_____

_____

_____

_____

_____

_____

_____

_____

_____

_____

_____

DAY
215

When beaten up by the uncertainty of life, we can give our birthright of seeing for ourselves away to a dominant parent or partner or to an orthodox tradition. —MARK NEPO

When uncertain about what to do regarding important matters, do you tend to let others decide for you? While this may be the easy way out, it is ceding some control of your life to them. Is this an issue for you? If so, how might you address it?

_____

_____

_____

_____

_____

_____

_____

_____

_____

_____

_____

_____

_____

_____

_____

_____

I'm not going to limit myself just because people won't accept the fact that I can do something else. —DOLLY PARTON

Write about a time when you did not allow other people to limit you and what resonates about the experience.

DAY 217

I don't ask myself, "Well, does God exist or does God not exist?" I choose to believe that God exists, and therefore I can say, "God, I can't do this by myself. Help me not to take a drink today. Help me not to take a drug today." And that works fine for me. —STEPHEN KING

How does your Higher Power help you?

_____

_____

_____

_____

_____

_____

_____

_____

_____

_____

_____

_____

_____

_____

_____

_____

_____

_____

Transformation happens over time by focusing on the little things with consistency. —DARI LUNA

What little things can you focus on consistently to further your inner transformation?

_____

_____

_____

_____

_____

_____

_____

_____

_____

_____

_____

_____

_____

_____

_____

_____

_____

You have the choice to believe that a thing is sacred and to know that you yourself are assigning that sacredness. There's such a specific human power in that. I love to think that there's this nothingness below it, and that we just pull from that and make whatever we want. And that's our magic as humans. —JACQUELINE SUSKIN

What feels most sacred to you and why?

_____

_____

_____

_____

_____

_____

_____

_____

_____

_____

_____

_____

_____

_____

_____

_____

_____

_____

*Matter is a captive moment in space and time, and by seeing our world and
ourselves materialistically, we make the captive aspects of the universe
assume too much importance.* —DEEPAK CHOPRA, MD

Among the things you own, which do you value the most and why? Do they
expand your inner peace or diminish it?

_____

_____

_____

_____

_____

_____

_____

_____

_____

_____

_____

_____

_____

_____

_____

_____

After the first play I was in, I was excited to read the reviews. There was one bad one, and that's all I remembered. I'd get up onstage every night and think about it. Since then, I never read about myself on the internet. I prefer to wake up feeling positive and put that out to the world. —JULIANNA MARGULIES

It is common for us to focus more on negative feedback than positive. Recount a time when you did that and how you might avoid repeating it.

_____

_____

_____

_____

_____

_____

_____

_____

_____

_____

_____

_____

_____

_____

_____

_____

_____

*To be baffled is not a comfortable position for us. We may even rush over it—
label it as "shock" and move on to "coping"—without looking at the deeper,
spiritual complexity (and holiness) that accompanies deep confusion. I'm
not positing we should remain in this period of perplexity indefinitely. But
I am suggesting to honor these moments of bewilderment, to hold them as
holy pauses that are rich with the potential for psychological and spiritual
awakening.* —DEBORAH ANNE QUIBELL

What profoundly baffles you and why? How could you explore it as an
opportunity for greater psychological and spiritual awakening?

_____

_____

_____

_____

_____

_____

_____

_____

_____

_____

_____

_____

_____

_____

DAY
223

Mindfulness reveals the unhappiness and turmoil that our inability to forgive causes us. We come to see that although it sometimes appears impossible, forgiveness would be a practical solution to some of the greatest suffering in our lives. —ROLF GATES

Remembering how you have been forgiven can create a foundation for you to forgive others. Journal about when you were forgiven for a significant mistake and how you might use what you learned from the experience to forgive others.

_____

_____

_____

_____

_____

_____

_____

_____

_____

_____

_____

_____

_____

_____

_____

_____

_____

_____

I surround myself with things that make me feel good: family, friends, walks, exercise. —MICHELLE OBAMA

What do you surround yourself with for self-care?

_____

_____

_____

_____

_____

_____

_____

_____

_____

_____

_____

_____

_____

_____

_____

_____

_____

_____

According to ancient Asian philosophy, life is not a circle but a spiral. Every life lesson that has ever been presented to you (which means everything you have ever been through) will come back again, in some form, until you learn it. —MARIANNE WILLIAMSON

What is a life lesson that keeps returning to you? What can help you learn it better?

_____

_____

_____

_____

_____

_____

_____

_____

_____

_____

_____

_____

_____

_____

_____

_____

_____

_____

Making the effort to hear someone else's viewpoint might not change our minds, but it can more fully inform our own judgment and help us better understand one another. —JAMES E. RYAN, JD

Reflect on a time that you disagreed with someone about an important issue. After taking a few mindful breaths, write about it from the other person's point of view to gain more insight.

_____

_____

_____

_____

_____

_____

_____

_____

_____

_____

_____

_____

_____

_____

_____

_____

Open your mouth and speak only when you are sure you can use calm and
loving speech. You have to train yourself to be able to do so. —THICH NHAT HANH

Journal about a time when you resisted the urge to speak because you were
too upset to do so calmly and lovingly. What resonates with you about this
experience?

_____

_____

_____

_____

_____

_____

_____

_____

_____

_____

_____

_____

_____

_____

_____

_____

_____

"I am worth it" is the rationalization phrase that seems to get us to set aside our sensibilities and do or buy stuff that we would have passed by if our wiser self was guiding us at that moment. It can place us in debtor's prison if we allow our debts to pile up, or we become chained to the work grind to support what we call our lifestyle. Often overconsumption leads to overwork, so that we have such little time that we allow buying experiences or stuff to compensate for our lack of time with ourselves and others. —PAUL SUTHERLAND

We all do it—buy stuff we do not need because we feel we deserve it. While this can be harmless, it can wreak havoc if we use this same rationalization to buy things beyond our means. Is this an issue for you? If so, how can you scale back on this?

_____

_____

_____

_____

_____

_____

_____

_____

_____

_____

_____

_____

_____

_____

Nature is and always will be my best friend. She is not constant or steady, but ever present. She is always there to soften a blow, to hold me, to teach me, to forgive me. She stays present when others go. She makes me laugh and cry and teaches me everything I need to know. —DELIA OWENS

What does nature do for you?

_____

_____

_____

_____

_____

_____

_____

_____

_____

_____

_____

_____

_____

_____

_____

_____

_____

_____

_____

You are a divine elephant with amnesia
trying to live in an ant hole. —HAFIZ

Without mindfulness, we can allow our minds to limit us and what we have to offer to the world. How have you practiced mindfulness lately and how can you do it more?

_____

_____

_____

_____

_____

_____

_____

_____

_____

_____

_____

_____

_____

_____

_____

_____

Setting boundaries and holding people accountable is a lot more work than shaming and blaming. But it's also more effective. —BRENÉ BROWN, PhD

How comfortable are you with setting firm boundaries with others, especially loved ones, and holding them accountable when they cross them? How can you become more comfortable with this?

_____

_____

_____

_____

_____

_____

_____

_____

_____

_____

_____

_____

_____

_____

_____

_____

_____

_____

_____

*The people I remember most are the ones who were kind to me when they did
not need to be.* —ROLF GATES

Who were these people for you? How might you "pay forward" their kindnesses
to others?

_____

_____

_____

_____

_____

_____

_____

_____

_____

_____

_____

_____

_____

_____

_____

_____

_____

_____

_____

DAY
233

Change for the better is still change, and so we need to ready ourselves for the good that comes our way as well as the bad. As always, it is the grounding of our lives with regular routines that makes it possible to handle any eventuality. —JULIA CAMERON

What are you doing to prepare yourself for change? Is it effective? If not, what other strategies might you try?

_____

_____

_____

_____

_____

_____

_____

_____

_____

_____

_____

_____

_____

_____

_____

_____

_____

When we're faced with a situation that we can't control or change with our current level of understanding and skill, evolutionary stress arises and impels us to question, seek, practice, and eventually take a leap outside our comfort zones into higher levels of consciousness. —SALLY KEMPTON

Journal about a situation that made you leap out of your comfort zone into a higher level of consciousness.

_____

_____

_____

_____

_____

_____

_____

_____

_____

_____

_____

_____

_____

_____

_____

_____

I practice being fully present and remember that all stress is caused by wanting this moment to be something it's not. I inhale what is. I accept this time for whatever it has to show me.

And I look for stillness beneath all the noise of the world, where everything is timeless. —OPRAH WINFREY

Where do you go to find stillness beneath all the noise of the world? How often do you go there? How might you do so more often?

_____

_____

_____

_____

_____

_____

_____

_____

_____

_____

_____

_____

_____

_____

_____

_____

Inner transformations can seem as slow as a tree branch growing. However, we need to consistently nurture ourselves, be patient, and let things unfold in their own way. —SHIVANI HAWKINS

What important changes are you trying to make? How can you be more patient with the process?

_____

_____

_____

_____

_____

_____

_____

_____

_____

_____

_____

_____

_____

_____

_____

_____

_____

DAY 237

If you're fed up with letting frustrations get the best of you, consider what every major world religion has to say about patience. Despite fiery disagreements about who or what God is and how to make contact, all these religions agree that patience is the essence of spirituality and thus grants great strength. —JUDITH ORLOFF, MD

What do you often get impatient with and why? How might you become more compassionate toward it?

_____

_____

_____

_____

_____

_____

_____

_____

_____

_____

_____

_____

_____

_____

_____

_____

_____

Knowing we can meet our own needs frees us to love without condition—and by staying open to love, we can drive ourselves sane. —MARTHA BECK

What is a recent need you had that you were able to meet on your own?

_____

_____

_____

_____

_____

_____

_____

_____

_____

_____

_____

_____

_____

_____

_____

_____

_____

_____

_____

_____

_____

The life of working really hard and being stressed and unhappy so that we can afford a vacation that we desperately need because our life is miserable ... doesn't make any sense. —BEN NUSSBAUM

Are there some things you do that—when you mindfully examine them—really do not make sense? If so, what are they? Use the space below to create a plan to abandon them.

_____

_____

_____

_____

_____

_____

_____

_____

_____

_____

_____

_____

_____

_____

_____

_____

_____

Be willing to see difficult people in a new way. Don't be so quick to believe that their behavior has anything to do with you. —IYANLA VANZANT

Do you have a person in your life who is difficult, if only occasionally? If so, how might their behavior be about them instead of you? Just increasing your awareness of this can help you avoid internalizing their negativity.

DAY 241

The best indicator of your level of consciousness is how you deal with life's challenges when they come. Through those challenges, an already unconscious person tends to become more deeply unconscious, and a conscious person more intensely conscious. You can use a challenge to awaken you, or you can allow it to pull you into even deeper sleep.
—ECKHART TOLLE

How did you react to your most recent major challenge? Would you change your reaction if it were to occur again? Why or why not?

Water,
wash me.
Earth,
support me.
Fire,
change me.
Wind,
carry me through. —LAURA HOPE-GILL

Looking back over the past week, who or what has helped carry you through?

_____

_____

_____

_____

_____

_____

_____

_____

_____

_____

_____

_____

_____

_____

_____

*If you circumambulated every holy shrine
in the world ten times,
It would not get you to heaven as quick
as controlling your anger.* —KABIR

Think about the most recent time you lost your temper. Why did you lose it and how can you avoid doing so in similar situations?

_____

_____

_____

_____

_____

_____

_____

_____

_____

_____

_____

_____

_____

_____

_____

_____

_____

Our society sets us up to think of abundance as money and things. But we can cultivate our own personal definition of what it means to have a bountiful life. —VICIE MORAN

What is your definition of a bountiful life? Are you living it? If not, develop a plan to do so with specific objectives and time frames.

_____

_____

_____

_____

_____

_____

_____

_____

_____

_____

_____

_____

_____

_____

_____

_____

_____

_____

No one has to be sucked into chaos and drama, but many have to learn this. —KAREN CASEY, PhD

Detail a time when you were able to resist getting sucked into other people's chaos and thus maintained your own peace of mind. How were you able to do this? How might you use those same skills now?

_____

_____

_____

_____

_____

_____

_____

_____

_____

_____

_____

_____

_____

_____

_____

_____

_____

_____

_____

_____

When you find yourself ruminating or feeling reactionary, pause, breathe, and say to yourself, "I might not be perceiving everything accurately right now." —RINA DESHPANDE

Detail the most recent time that you stressed yourself by misperceiving a circumstance. What led to your misperception and what can you learn from the experience?

_____

_____

_____

_____

_____

_____

_____

_____

_____

_____

_____

_____

_____

_____

_____

_____

Live below your means, but within your needs. —SUZE ORMAN

Financial stress can take a heavy toll on your health, relationships, and other important aspects of your life. Do you live below your means but within your needs? If not, what is the first step to change this?

As you make a habit of not taking anything personally, you won't need to place your trust in what others do or say. You will only need to trust yourself to make responsible choices. —DON MIGUEL RUIZ

What pivotal choices do you trust yourself to make and why?

_____

_____

_____

_____

_____

_____

_____

_____

_____

_____

_____

_____

_____

_____

_____

_____

_____

_____

DAY 249

Minds can be limiting. Especially when they tell us we're not steady enough to hold Handstand, strong enough to hike to a summit, or creative enough to come up with solutions when we feel stuck. But we don't have to listen.
—DJ TOWNSEL

Do you frequently have thoughts that limit you? If so, which are the most common ones? Take a few minutes to practice watching them move across your awareness like mist, then journal about how you feel.

_____

_____

_____

_____

_____

_____

_____

_____

_____

_____

_____

_____

_____

_____

_____

_____

_____

*Many of us learned early to react to life and circumstances rather
than to act on our own behalf. We learned to let other people's behavior
determine how we were going to feel about ourselves. Making a conscious
choice to act and not react takes forethought. It takes willingness to be more
responsible for ourselves and a commitment to remaining independent of,
not dependent on, the opinions of others to establish the sum and substance
of who we are.* —KAREN CASEY, PhD

A major step toward emotional independence from others' opinions about us
is recognizing times that we allowed those opinions to undermine our authentic
selves. Recount a time when you did this, or were tempted to, to help avoid
repeating this.

_____

_____

_____

_____

_____

_____

_____

_____

_____

_____

_____

_____

Any pain or disease you have is like an island of discomfort surrounded by an ocean of comfort, for in comparison to any one disease, your healthy awareness is as big as an ocean. —DEEPAK CHOPRA, MD

Focusing on what is wrong with our bodies makes us lose sight of what is right with them. List at least five positive aspects of your current state of health.

_____

_____

_____

_____

_____

_____

_____

_____

_____

_____

_____

_____

_____

_____

_____

_____

_____

I'm driven because I haven't achieved everything. When I've achieved all my ambitions, then I guess that I will have done it and I can just say "great." But I'm still hungry. I want it. I've still got the burning fire that burns brightly inside of me. . . . I still have many rivers to cross! —JIMMY CLIFF

What is an important goal you have yet to achieve? Why is it important? At what point are you in achieving this goal? What else do you need to accomplish it and what is the time frame for doing so?

DAY 253

Those events and people in our lives who trigger our unresolved issues could be regarded as good news. We don't have to go hunting for anything. We don't need to try to create situations in which we reach our limit. They occur all by themselves, with clockwork regularity. —PEMA CHÖDRÖN

Are there events or people who trigger unresolved issues for you? If so, what and who are they and what unresolved issues do they trigger? How can you address them better?

_____

_____

_____

_____

_____

_____

_____

_____

_____

_____

_____

_____

_____

_____

_____

_____

_____

_____

Each one of us has an essential role in the whole of humanity. All you have to do is follow your path to answer the call. —OPRAH WINFREY

How have you been following your path to answer your call?

_____

_____

_____

_____

_____

_____

_____

_____

_____

_____

_____

_____

_____

_____

_____

_____

_____

_____

_____

_____

DAY 255

One of the best ways I've found to understand people whose lives are different from mine is to be of service. Through my work with Alzheimer's, volunteering at Special Olympics and Best Buddies, and in service opportunities at my church—I have felt fulfilled, I have felt connected, and I have felt that I understand other people in ways I couldn't have otherwise. —MARIA SHRIVER

In what ways have you been of service to people different from yourself and how did that increase your understanding of them? If you feel the need for more opportunities to do this, create an action plan to achieve this goal.

_____

_____

_____

_____

_____

_____

_____

_____

_____

_____

_____

_____

_____

_____

I realized that one isn't born with courage. One develops it by doing small courageous things—in the way that if one sets out to pick up a 100-pound bag of rice, one would be advised to start with a five-pound bag, then 10 pounds, then 20 pounds, and so forth, until one builds up enough muscle to lift the 100-pound bag. It's the same way with courage. You do small courageous things that require some mental and spiritual exertion.
—MAYA ANGELOU

Do a small courageous thing and journal about the experience. How can you build upon your success with this?

Mrs. Chase believes in a God who has all the answers, and really wants what's best for her. This is a bold statement coming from a woman who grew up in a segregated country that would not allow her to vote or mix too much with white people. She is a woman who watched her city and Dooky Chase, the restaurant where she had been cooking for more than sixty years, drown mostly due to a greedy and corrupt government. But still she has faith. And she has the kind of faith I longed for: one that had been tested. —KIM SEVERSON

In her memoir, *Spoon Fed: How Eight Cooks Saved My Life*, food writer Kim Severson devotes a chapter to this acclaimed New Orleans restaurateur who exemplified how hardships can test and strengthen spiritual faith.

Recount a time when your faith was tested and strengthened.

_____

_____

_____

_____

_____

_____

_____

_____

_____

_____

_____

_____

_____

The real you is still a little child who never grew up. Sometimes that little child comes out when you are having fun or playing, when you feel happy, when you are painting, or writing poetry, or playing the piano, or expressing yourself in some way. These are the happiest moments of your life—when the real you comes out, when you don't care about the past and you don't worry about the future. —DON MIGUEL RUIZ

Do something fun—singing, drawing, coloring—whatever comes to mind, then write about the experience.

Spirituality affects our work in three key areas: It leads us to engage in work that gives life meaning; it calls on us to do work that is ethical and carried out in an ethical context; and it inspires us to do work that makes a contribution to society. If you use these three criteria in choosing a life work, the possibilities quickly get narrowed and you are on your way toward work that suits you. —THOMAS MOORE

Are you either in or on your way to work that suits you? If not, create a specific plan to change this.

_____

_____

_____

_____

_____

_____

_____

_____

_____

_____

_____

_____

_____

_____

_____

_____

*The discomfort associated with groundlessness, with the fundamental
ambiguity of being human, comes from our attachment to wanting things
to be a certain way.* —PEMA CHÖDRÖN

What things do you want a certain way? How do you respond when they are not?
Is this a response you would benefit from changing? Why or why not?

_____

_____

_____

_____

_____

_____

_____

_____

_____

_____

_____

_____

_____

_____

_____

_____

*If you can't feel relaxed in a clean and tidy room, try confronting your
feeling of anxiety. It may shed light on what is really bothering you. When
your room is clean and uncluttered, you have no choice but to examine
your inner state. You can see any issues you have been avoiding and are
forced to deal with them.* —MARIE KONDO

Thoroughly clean a room in your home, then breathe mindfully for a few minutes
and journal about any issues still weighing on your mind and how you might
address them.

_____

_____

_____

_____

_____

_____

_____

_____

_____

_____

_____

_____

_____

_____

_____

People are full of fear and suffering, and laughing makes us feel better.
—ROLF GATES

When you find yourself in the grip of unsettling emotions, what helps you to laugh and feel better?

_____

_____

_____

_____

_____

_____

_____

_____

_____

_____

_____

_____

_____

_____

_____

_____

_____

_____

You are responsible only for making the effort, nothing more.
—KAREN CASEY, PHD

There are times when our best efforts do not produce the results we want. If we focus on the result, we feel like failures, but if we focus on our efforts, we feel like successes.

Use the space below to transform a failure into a success by detailing how hard you tried to make it work.

Jesus said, "If you hold to my teaching, you are really my disciples. Then you will know the truth, and the truth will set you free." —JOHN 8:31–32

Which truth has been most freeing for you and why?

_____

_____

_____

_____

_____

_____

_____

_____

_____

_____

_____

_____

_____

_____

_____

_____

_____

_____

_____

_____

My whole life, comedy has been a tool I've used to process pain. —TREVOR NOAH

What do you use to process pain? How well does it work? If it's not effective
enough, what other ways might you try?

_____

_____

_____

_____

_____

_____

_____

_____

_____

_____

_____

_____

_____

_____

_____

_____

_____

_____

_____

Anger isn't the most popular emotion. We often get the message that we should focus on compassion and forgiveness, and that anger is somehow not a spiritual emotion. But trying to paste over our rage with forgiveness can literally make us sick. When we learn how to work with our anger, it can not only help us navigate our intimate relationships, it can teach us who we are and what really matters to us. Our rage can light our way in the dark.
—JULIE PETERS

Begin the journey from anger to compassion and forgiveness by using the space below to specify why a certain behavior was wrong and how it hurt you. Then identify ways to address it. For example, calmly tell a family member why what they did was hurtful and how you want them to make amends. Regardless of the response, you will be successful by simply asserting yourself.

*As the movement patterns of each breath—inhalation, exhalation, lull—are
observed as to duration, number, and area of focus, breath becomes spacious
and subtle.* —PATANJALI

Focusing on the breath is an effective way to quiet our often unruly minds. Settle
yourself comfortably in a quiet place, close your eyes, and as you breathe in,
slowly count to 4; pause for a moment, and as you breathe out, lengthen your
breath to the count of 8, and pause once again. Repeat this cycle for several
minutes, then journal how you feel.

_____

_____

_____

_____

_____

_____

_____

_____

_____

_____

_____

_____

_____

_____

_____

Good poetry, the kind that pierces your soul with wonder and truth, makes me feel less alone. —ELIZABETH MARGLIN

What makes you feel less alone and why?

_____

_____

_____

_____

_____

_____

_____

_____

_____

_____

_____

_____

_____

_____

_____

_____

_____

_____

I wake up before the sun rises because I like to watch it rise. By observing nature, I can feel a life force. I look outside my window to the sky and tell myself this is going to be the best day of my life. —TAO PORCHON-LYNCH

What helps get your day off to its best start? How might you increase the frequency of doing this?

_____

_____

_____

_____

_____

_____

_____

_____

_____

_____

_____

_____

_____

_____

_____

_____

_____

Wherever you go you will find people lying to you, and as your awareness grows, you will notice that you also lie to yourself. —DON MIGUEL RUIZ

DAY
270

What do you tend to lie to yourself about and why?

_____

_____

_____

_____

_____

_____

_____

_____

_____

_____

_____

_____

_____

_____

_____

_____

_____

_____

_____

DAY
271

It takes five alarms, coffee, my husband yelling at me, and my cat sitting on my chest before I get out of bed. But I will exercise first thing in the morning because it helps me deal with my anxiety. If I don't, my natural temperament controls me—exercise makes me braver. —KELLY McGONIGAL, PhD

What makes you braver? How might you make it more part of your daily routine?

_____

_____

_____

_____

_____

_____

_____

_____

_____

_____

_____

_____

_____

_____

_____

_____

_____

_____

Losing my mother—as painful as it was—has brought a blessing I could not have anticipated. It has led me to realign my sense of focus, my values, my attention. —MARGARET O'ROURKE

If we focus only on our grief after the death of a loved one, we can miss blessings from that loss that can help us improve our lives. What is a blessing you have, or can gain, from the loss of someone you cherished?

_____

_____

_____

_____

_____

_____

_____

_____

_____

_____

_____

_____

_____

_____

_____

_____

_____

Rationalizing keeps us safe in our own little bubble world, saying "na, na, na, na..." to drown out anything that might cause us to actually change or admit we were or are wrong. —PAUL SUTHERLAND

Recount a time when you admitted you were wrong about an important issue and another time that you did the opposite. What are the lessons from both experiences?

_____

_____

_____

_____

_____

_____

_____

_____

_____

_____

_____

_____

_____

_____

_____

_____

_____

_____

I truly believe that every day brings a new hope. We get to start again, and try again, and be grateful all over again. —AVA DuVERNAY

What is a new hope for you and why?

_____

_____

_____

_____

_____

_____

_____

_____

_____

_____

_____

_____

_____

_____

_____

_____

_____

_____

DAY 275

When we judge, we get an instant hit of self-righteousness, but subconsciously we know we're separating ourselves from who we really are: compassionate, kind people. As a result, we feel guilty once our high wears off—and to avoid that feeling, we have to judge someone else. This cycle weakens us mentally and physically. —GABRIELLE BERNSTEIN

Our minds are hardwired to make judgments about everything, especially other people, in ways that create needless negativity. The first step to counteracting this unproductive tendency is to increase your awareness of it. Who do you tend to judge and why?

_____

_____

_____

_____

_____

_____

_____

_____

_____

_____

_____

_____

_____

_____

_____

_____

_____

The inner intelligence of the body is the ultimate and supreme genius in nature. It mirrors the wisdom of the cosmos. —VEDIC VERSE

Settle into a comfortable position and follow your breath as it moves through you, paying special attention to its coolness as you breathe in and its warmth as you release it. Next, check in with your body. What is it telling you?

_____

_____

_____

_____

_____

_____

_____

_____

_____

_____

_____

_____

_____

_____

_____

_____

_____

_____

_____

DAY
277

I want to understand why I might act in ways that don't reflect the person I want to be—so that I become more accountable. —JAMES HOLLIS, PhD

Journal about a significant time when how you behaved did not reflect the person you strive to be. What most resonates with you about this?

_____

_____

_____

_____

_____

_____

_____

_____

_____

_____

_____

_____

_____

_____

_____

_____

_____

_____

_____

When we are stressed, our initial thoughts often present themselves as the last word on the situation. If we lose a job we might think: I failed. But we could choose to pause and add to that: I failed to find my authentic self in that work. —KEVIN ANDERSON, PhD

First write of a negative thought you recently had about yourself, then add to it as exemplified above to transform it into something positive.

_____

_____

_____

_____

_____

_____

_____

_____

_____

_____

_____

_____

_____

_____

_____

_____

DAY
279

Your mistakes can also lead you to the Truth. —RUMI

What is a mistake you made that led you to discover something important?

It is important for us to travel, to meet people who seem different from us. You realize that they aren't that different. We are all together on this planet, and we need to be working together more. —JOSÉ ANDRÉS

What has been your most enlightening trip and why?

_____

_____

_____

_____

_____

_____

_____

_____

_____

_____

_____

_____

_____

_____

_____

_____

_____

DAY
281

Take care of each moment and you will take care of all time.
—BUDDHIST PROVERB

How are you taking care of this moment, the only one you have to truly live?

_____

_____

_____

_____

_____

_____

_____

_____

_____

_____

_____

_____

_____

_____

_____

_____

_____

_____

_____

This is what spiritual development means—the recognition, realization, and manifestation of the Spirit within us. —THE *KYBALION*

What is helping you develop spiritually and how?

_____

_____

_____

_____

_____

_____

_____

_____

_____

_____

_____

_____

_____

_____

_____

_____

_____

_____

_____

_____

_____

When I sing, I get a feeling of connection to something else—something bigger. When I tap into it, there's nothing like it. It's just complete bliss.
—BELINDA CARLISLE

What gives you a connection to something bigger than yourself and why?

_____

_____

_____

_____

_____

_____

_____

_____

_____

_____

_____

_____

_____

_____

_____

_____

_____

_____

_____

_____

We think anger is bad and grief is too painful. But anything that is going on in your system is potent and revealing something to you. This includes awful sensations, anxiety, grief, and anger. You may experience a primal rage that is telling you that a boundary was crossed or a really deep need or want is not being met. This is amazing information that can guide and inform the changes or new actions you need to take. —SHIVANI HAWKINS

What emotions have you experienced lately? Are they revealing some action or changes you need to make to improve your life? If so, how will you follow through?

DAY
285

*We are meant to be in relationships. We are always in a relationship, with
ourselves, our environment—even the solitary mystic on the mountain is in
a relationship with life, breath, and the cosmos. We need each other.*
—PAUL SUTHERLAND

Who do you need and why? Who needs you and why?

_____

_____

_____

_____

_____

_____

_____

_____

_____

_____

_____

_____

_____

_____

_____

_____

The breeze at dawn has secrets to tell you.
Don't go back to sleep!
You must ask for what you really want.
Don't go back to sleep!
People are going back and forth across the doorsill
where the two worlds touch.
The door is round and open.
Don't go back to sleep! —RUMI

Are there some important things that you have become oblivious to? If so, what are they?

_____

_____

_____

_____

_____

_____

_____

_____

_____

_____

_____

_____

_____

_____

DAY 287

Some people are driven by the past: "I've always been this way!" So they can't see themselves in a new way. —RICK WARREN

What is a helpful new way you can see yourself?

_____

_____

_____

_____

_____

_____

_____

_____

_____

_____

_____

_____

_____

_____

_____

_____

_____

_____

How great is the love the Father has lavished on us, that we should be called children of God! And that is what we are! —1 JOHN 3:1

Do your actions reflect that you are a beloved child of God? Why or why not? If they do not, how can you change this?

_____

_____

_____

_____

_____

_____

_____

_____

_____

_____

_____

_____

_____

_____

_____

_____

_____

_____

_____

_____

The greatest gift we can give ourselves is to accept love in all its forms, and learn to give ourselves whatever love we didn't receive. —OPRAH WINFREY

How do you accept love? Does it have to be from certain people or specific conditions? How do you give yourself love that you have not received?

_____

_____

_____

_____

_____

_____

_____

_____

_____

_____

_____

_____

_____

_____

_____

_____

_____

_____

_____

_____

Returning hate for hate only multiplies hate, adding deeper darkness to a night already devoid of stars. Darkness cannot drive out darkness; only light can do that. Hate cannot drive out hate; only love can do that. Hate multiplies hate, violence multiplies violence, and toughness multiplies toughness in a descending spiral of destruction. —DR. MARTIN LUTHER KING, JR.

Think of someone you often have conflicts with and imagine that person as your young, precious child. Use the space below to write a compassionate note to that child.

_____

_____

_____

_____

_____

_____

_____

_____

_____

_____

_____

_____

_____

_____

_____

_____

Through my journey, I've learned so much, but one thing always stands out the most: Obstacles you face on your path do not put a halt to your progress— they teach you how to climb. —DJ TOWNSEL

Which obstacles have you faced that most taught you how to climb? How did they do that?

_____

_____

_____

_____

_____

_____

_____

_____

_____

_____

_____

_____

_____

_____

_____

_____

_____

_____

For too long I'd been waiting for the wonderful. But there is so much joy in everyday occurrences: a butterfly in the sun, the first crisp bite of an apple, the rich aroma of roasting meat. Maybe I had to break my foot to open my eyes, but I finally understood why cooking means so much to me. In a world filled with no, it is my yes. —RUTH REICHL

Physical setbacks can offer blessings if we are willing to see them with fresh eyes. What is a physical condition you had or have now that you can reframe into something uplifting?

_____

_____

_____

_____

_____

_____

_____

_____

_____

_____

_____

_____

_____

_____

_____

DAY
293

I can well remember my childhood refrain, "He made me do it." Whenever I did something punishable but wanted to avoid getting spanked, I would just foist the blame onto my younger brother. Seldom did it work, of course, which was lucky for my brother. But I was slow to learn that blaming others was more than just wrong; it was dishonest, disrespectful, and dehumanizing; most of all, it prevented me from achieving the growth I deserved and could only get through taking responsibility for my own actions. —KAREN CASEY, PhD

Is there someone in the past or present whom you blame for something you did? If so, who is it and what do you blame them for? How can you shift your perception of this to achieve more personal growth?

_____

_____

_____

_____

_____

_____

_____

_____

_____

_____

_____

_____

_____

_____

_____

_____

Any cell, tissue, or organ is capable of crying out for attention, and when you give it some, the healing process begins. —DEEPAK CHOPRA, MD

What have you been doing lately to improve your physical health?

_____

_____

_____

_____

_____

_____

_____

_____

_____

_____

_____

_____

_____

_____

_____

_____

_____

_____

_____

_____

_____

Music, at its essence, is what gives us memories. And the longer a song has existed in our lives, the more memories we have of it. —STEVIE WONDER

What are your most memorable songs and how do you feel when you hear them?

_____

_____

_____

_____

_____

_____

_____

_____

_____

_____

_____

_____

_____

_____

_____

_____

_____

_____

_____

_____

Perfectionism is not self-improvement. Perfectionism is, at its core, about trying to earn approval and acceptance. Most perfectionists were raised being praised for achievement and performance (grades, manners, rule-following, people-pleasing, appearance, sports). Somewhere along the way, we adopt this dangerous and debilitating belief system: I am what I accomplish and how well I accomplish it. Please. Perform. Perfect. *Healthy striving is self-focused—*How can I improve? *Perfectionism is other-focused—*What will they think? —BRENÉ BROWN, PhD

Remember a time when your striving was self-focused and another when it was other-focused. What are the lessons from both experiences?

DAY
297

Several years ago, I found myself having to re-create my own life. I had to step into the unknown and sit there. It was terrifying. I can't tell you I enjoyed it, but I can say I learned that I could re-imagine, re-construct, and re-build my life. And every day I continue to do it. —MARIA SHRIVER

Has there been a point in your life when you had to step into the unknown to re-create your life? If so, when was it and how did you accomplish it? How might those same skills serve you now?

_____

_____

_____

_____

_____

_____

_____

_____

_____

_____

_____

_____

_____

_____

_____

_____

_____

_____

The deep uncertainty that arises during processes of change is perhaps the most daunting part of the experience. Why? Because a true change process will involve surprises, reversals, false starts, and periods of coming to a dead halt. —SALLY KEMPTON

Describe the stages of a major change you experienced and what you learned from each stage.

_____

_____

_____

_____

_____

_____

_____

_____

_____

_____

_____

_____

_____

_____

_____

_____

_____

DAY 299

Often we think of the people we don't like as our enemies, but in fact, they're all-important to us. They're our greatest teachers: special messengers who show up just when we need them, to point out our fixed identity. —PEMA CHÖDRÖN

What are the most important things your "enemies" have taught you about yourself and how did they do that?

_____

_____

_____

_____

_____

_____

_____

_____

_____

_____

_____

_____

_____

_____

_____

_____

Studying and being trained in the philosophy and discipline of nonviolence, it helped to make me stronger, wiser, gave me a greater sense of determination, and if it hadn't been for my coming under the influence of Martin Luther King Jr., James Lawson, and wonderful colleagues, students, the young people . . . I don't think I would have survived the beatings, the arrests. —REPRESENTATIVE JOHN LEWIS

What has been helping you survive and how?

_____

_____

_____

_____

_____

_____

_____

_____

_____

_____

_____

_____

_____

_____

_____

_____

DAY
301

Stories appear in our minds hundreds of times a day—when someone gets up without a word and walks out of the room, when someone doesn't smile or doesn't return a phone call. . . . Stories are the untested, uninvestigated theories that tell us what all these things mean. We don't even realize that they're just theories. —BYRON KATIE

What was a recent story you told yourself that was not based on reality? What led to your creation of it and what can you learn from this experience?

You were born with the right to be happy. You were born with the right to love, to enjoy and to share your love. You are alive, so take your life and enjoy it. Don't resist life passing through you, because that is God passing through you. Just your existence proves the existence of God. Your existence proves the existence of life and energy. —DON MIGUEL RUIZ

How are you exercising your right to enjoy life?

DAY
303

No matter what path I have taken to the moment in my life, I can change it as I change my thoughts. —MARIANNE WILLIAMSON

Recount a time that you changed course regarding a substantial issue after learning more about it. What resonates with you about this?

_____

_____

_____

_____

_____

_____

_____

_____

_____

_____

_____

_____

_____

_____

_____

_____

_____

_____

_____

_____

When I sense myself filling with rage at the absence of a beloved, I try as soon as possible to remember that my concerns and questions, my efforts and answers should be focused on what I did or can learn from my departed love. What legacy was left which can help me in the art of living a good life? —MAYA ANGELOU

The pain of losing loved ones can be eased if we remember important lessons they taught us. Who have been those people for you and what did they teach you? Have you applied those lessons? If not yet, how might you?

_____

_____

_____

_____

_____

_____

_____

_____

_____

_____

_____

_____

_____

_____

DAY
305

We return to the mountains
For peace
And to remember
That some part of us
Soars above the sun. —LAURA HOPE-GILL

Which place has recently offered solace to you and how did it do that?

_____

_____

_____

_____

_____

_____

_____

_____

_____

_____

_____

_____

_____

_____

_____

_____

_____

*Here is the incredible benefit of taking a leap: It strengthens your ability
to keep returning to your core faith in what you hold dear. Think of it as a
virtuous cycle, instead of a vicious one. You take risks based on your beliefs,
and the happy results of those risks bolster your beliefs. Those convictions
don't just determine how courageous you are. They also determine how
joyful and satisfied you are, every day of your life.* —HEATHER HAVRILESKY

What is an important leap of faith you have taken that has strengthened your
core beliefs and how did it do that?

_____

_____

_____

_____

_____

_____

_____

_____

_____

_____

_____

_____

_____

_____

DAY
307

Impermanence teaches us to respect and value every moment and all the precious things around us and inside of us. When we practice mindfulness of impermanence, we become fresher and more loving. —THICH NHAT HANH

Journal about a time when you not only accepted but also embraced the impermanence in life. What did you learn from this experience?

_____

_____

_____

_____

_____

_____

_____

_____

_____

_____

_____

_____

_____

_____

_____

_____

_____

_____

Remember that the word passion *comes from the Latin* patior, *which means to suffer. More people suffer from disconnects from their souls than any other trauma.* —JAMES HOLLIS, PhD

In a culture that seems bent on disconnecting us from our souls, how do you reconnect to yours and how often do you do it?

DAY
309

If we have learned to tap into a source of compassion larger than our small selves—call it Compassion, Love, Source, God—that abundant energy wants to fill us and spill over to others. This allows us to give compassionate presence not from depletion or self-sacrifice but from continual replenishment. —KEVIN ANDERSON, PhD

How do you tap into a source of compassion greater than yourself and thus give it to others from continual replenishment instead?

I've also learned that I have to stop doing things that block joy. I have to keep turning off that inner voice of critical self-judgment and shame, stop avoiding living in the present by overly focusing on the future, stop numbing myself with cookies and ice cream. —MARIA SHRIVER

Do you have habits that block joy? If so, what are they?

_____

_____

_____

_____

_____

_____

_____

_____

_____

_____

_____

_____

_____

_____

_____

_____

_____

_____

DAY 311

We tend to identify with our thoughts to an even greater extent than we do with our bodies. When we're feeling blue and thinking lots of sorrowful thoughts, we say to ourselves, I am a sad person. But if we bang our funny bone, we don't usually say to ourselves, I am a sore elbow. Most of the time, we think we are our thoughts.

We forget, or have never noticed, that there's an aspect of our mind that's watching these thoughts arise and pass away. —SHARON SALZBERG

Find a place where you will not be disturbed for about ten minutes. Start scanning your body with gentle awareness, starting with the top of your head, then moving to the soles of your feet, simply noticing any sensations without trying to change them. Next, journal how you feel.

_____

_____

_____

_____

_____

_____

_____

_____

_____

_____

_____

_____

_____

You are woven from nature and your system is constantly trying to
repair itself with or without your help. It's your job to support the natural
process. Each day you can discover something new or make a small
change. —SHIVANI HAWKINS

What is something you can do, however small, to help repair yourself emotionally, physically, or spiritually?

_____

_____

_____

_____

_____

_____

_____

_____

_____

_____

_____

_____

_____

_____

_____

_____

_____

Distraction is the great enemy of enjoyment. When we're distracted, we're liable to substitute quantity for quality, reaching for another helping or another stimulant or a different body because we haven't been present enough to fully enjoy what we have. —SALLY KEMPTON

What are frequent distractions for you, things that keep you from fully engaging in the present moment? How might you reduce their pull on you?

_____

_____

_____

_____

_____

_____

_____

_____

_____

_____

_____

_____

_____

_____

_____

_____

_____

When you go into the cold water, you're no longer thinking about your mortgage, your next meal, your emotional baggage. You're not caught up in your thoughts. It's freezing, and you're just surviving. That brought me to a place where I could heal. —WIM HOF

What is a physical activity that helps heal your mind? How can you engage in it more often?

_____

_____

_____

_____

_____

_____

_____

_____

_____

_____

_____

_____

_____

_____

_____

_____

DAY 315

It's a simple and generous rule of life that whatever you practice, you will improve at. For instance: If I had spent my twenties playing basketball every single day, or making pastry dough every single day, or studying auto mechanics every single day, I'd probably be good at foul shots and croissants and transmissions by now.

Instead, I learned how to write. —ELIZABETH GILBERT

What is something you would benefit from practicing routinely to get better at? Detail a plan to do so.

_____

_____

_____

_____

_____

_____

_____

_____

_____

_____

_____

_____

_____

_____

_____

_____

Sweet friendships refresh the soul. —PROVERBS 27:9

Which friendship has nourished you recently and how?

We're free to think and go in any direction we want in this information age, and we have to protect our ears, our eyes, our minds. We have to be very careful with the information we take in and rely on as truth.
—DENZEL WASHINGTON

Through everything from social media to cable news networks, our culture tries to inundate us with information, but much of it is untrue and causes unnecessary suffering. How do you protect yourself from this? Is it enough?

_____

_____

_____

_____

_____

_____

_____

_____

_____

_____

_____

_____

_____

_____

_____

_____

Being in touch with your needs is the most powerful way to be in touch with where your inner intelligence is heading at any given moment. This attentiveness makes you a conscious person, someone who is evolving along lines no one else will exactly duplicate, not even the greatest of the masters. —DEEPAK CHOPRA, MD

What do you truly need in your life now? Why do you need it? Is this need (or are these needs) being met? If not, how can you change this?

_____

_____

_____

_____

_____

_____

_____

_____

_____

_____

_____

_____

_____

_____

_____

_____

And I do believe that the darkness is where we learn to see. That is when we see ourselves clearer—when there is no light. —BONO

What have you learned about yourself during the darkest periods of your life?

_____

_____

_____

_____

_____

_____

_____

_____

_____

_____

_____

_____

_____

_____

_____

_____

_____

_____

_____

With increased inner strength it is possible to develop firm determination and with determination there is a greater chance of success, no matter what obstacles there may be. —DALAI LAMA XIV

You have inner strength. What helped you develop it and how can you build upon it?

_____

_____

_____

_____

_____

_____

_____

_____

_____

_____

_____

_____

_____

_____

_____

_____

_____

_____

_____

DAY
321

Who of you by worrying can add a single hour to your life? —MATTHEW 6:27

What have you been worrying about lately and why? Set aside ten minutes in a quiet, comfortable place and practice watching your worries in a compassionate manner as they move through your awareness and disappear into nothingness.

_____

_____

_____

_____

_____

_____

_____

_____

_____

_____

_____

_____

_____

_____

_____

_____

_____

_____

I can't put it any more simply or emphatically: How we behave toward our money, how we treat our money, speaks volumes about how we perceive and value ourselves. —SUZE ORMAN

What does the way you treat your money say about you? If it is something you want to change, come up with specific objectives with timelines for accomplishing them.

_____

_____

_____

_____

_____

_____

_____

_____

_____

_____

_____

_____

_____

_____

_____

_____

_____

DAY 323

Just as we habitually hoard old birthday cards and souvenirs, bank statements and receipts, clothes, broken appliances and old magazines, we also hang on to pride, anger, outdated opinions and fear. —TIMBER HAWKEYE

What have you been hanging on to lately that you would benefit from letting go of and why?

_____

_____

_____

_____

_____

_____

_____

_____

_____

_____

_____

_____

_____

_____

_____

_____

_____

_____

_____

I feel like many forms of exercise teach us how not to suffer alone. And I believe that's true even if you exercise alone, because ultimately it changes your neurochemistry. —KELLY McGONIGAL, PhD

Whether it is taking an aerobics class or taking a brisk walk around your neighborhood, any form of physical exercise increases your brain's production of dopamine, serotonin, and other neurochemicals that give you a sense of well-being and improved ability to interact with others. What is your favorite form of exercise? How often do you do it? If it is less than three times a week, how can you make time to exercise more often?

_____

_____

_____

_____

_____

_____

_____

_____

_____

_____

_____

_____

_____

_____

_____

DAY
325

In the silence of our hearts, God speaks of His love. —MOTHER TERESA

What is the Divine telling you now?

Integrity is doing the right thing when you don't have to—when no one else is looking or will ever know. —CHARLES MARSHALL

When was the most significant time that you acted with integrity? What empowered you to do so?

_____

_____

_____

_____

_____

_____

_____

_____

_____

_____

_____

_____

_____

_____

_____

_____

_____

_____

_____

DAY 327

Run, my dear, from anything
that may not strengthen
your precious, budding wings. —HAFIZ

What are things—or people—who often drain you? How might you lessen their
ability to affect you like this?

_____

_____

_____

_____

_____

_____

_____

_____

_____

_____

_____

_____

_____

_____

_____

_____

_____

_____

Happiness is not a station you arrive at, but a manner of traveling.
—MARGARET LEE RUNBECK

How are you traveling on your journey toward happiness? What is helping you?
What is hindering you, and how might you overcome it?

_____

_____

_____

_____

_____

_____

_____

_____

_____

_____

_____

_____

_____

_____

_____

_____

_____

_____

_____

_____

DAY
329

Invent your world. Surround yourself with people, color, sounds, and work that nourish you. —SARK

What has nourished you lately and why?

_____

_____

_____

_____

_____

_____

_____

_____

_____

_____

_____

_____

_____

_____

_____

_____

_____

_____

_____

_____

_____

I am not a product of my circumstances. I am a product of my decisions.
—STEPHEN COVEY

What are your major decisions that shaped your life and what have you learned from them?

_____

_____

_____

_____

_____

_____

_____

_____

_____

_____

_____

_____

_____

_____

One of my biggest aha moments was . . . noticing that everything you need is pointless if you don't take the initiative to enjoy it. —KAUI HART HEMMINGS

How do you enjoy what you have?

_____

_____

_____

_____

_____

_____

_____

_____

_____

_____

_____

_____

_____

_____

_____

_____

_____

_____

_____

_____

_____

_____

My ego would prefer I avoid the pain, and not look too closely at the root of its cause. Today I choose the courage it takes to look honestly at who I've been, how I've behaved, and how I've contributed to the problems that beset my life. —MARIANNE WILLIAMSON

Take a compassionate yet honest look at yourself and journal about how you have contributed to the problems that beset you. What lessons appear that you can use to improve your life?

_____

_____

_____

_____

_____

_____

_____

_____

_____

_____

_____

_____

_____

_____

_____

_____

DAY
333

While no one can live your life for you, we're woefully deficient of the wisdom necessary to live, if left to our experience alone. Just as we can't see unless our eyes are open, we need the experience and company of others to open our deeper mind, though we're left to do the seeing for ourselves. —MARK NEPO

Whose experience have you gained wisdom from, whether it is someone in your life now or someone who lived thousands of years ago? What has their experience taught you?

_____

_____

_____

_____

_____

_____

_____

_____

_____

_____

_____

_____

_____

_____

_____

_____

It's possible to feel both bad and move on. It requires that we practice both/ and thinking rather than either/or: "Yes, I feel terrible about losing my house and *I can make where I'm renting as pleasant as possible"; "Yes, I made financial mistakes* and *I'm still a responsible person." Cultivating the ability to hold both beliefs helps us to experience our feelings* and *rebound, and is one of the foundations of wisdom.* —M. J. RYAN

Which issues would you benefit from practicing "both/and" thinking instead of "either/or"?

DAY 335

The primary cause of unhappiness is never the situation but your thoughts about it. Be aware of the thoughts you are thinking. Separate them from the situation, which is always neutral, which always is as it is. There is the situation or the fact, and here are my thoughts about it. Instead of making up stories, stay with the facts. For example, "I am ruined" is a story. It limits you and prevents you from taking effective action. "I have fifty cents left in my bank account" is a fact. Facing facts is always empowering. —ECKHART TOLLE

Think of something you are unhappy about. Write your perceptions of it, then the facts about it. Did this activity change how you feel about the circumstance? Why or why not?

_____

_____

_____

_____

_____

_____

_____

_____

_____

_____

_____

_____

_____

*It's easier to look back than it is ahead. But that's where your mission is
waiting for you, and that's where you've got to look.* —CHIEF LEON SHENANDOAH

What are you most looking forward to and why?

_____

_____

_____

_____

_____

_____

_____

_____

_____

_____

_____

_____

_____

_____

_____

_____

_____

_____

_____

_____

_____

There are two ways to live. One is as though nothing is a miracle. The other is as though everything is a miracle. —ALBERT EINSTEIN

You are experiencing miracles today. You woke up this morning while millions of people around the world did not. You can read these words while millions are illiterate. You can write your ideas, feelings, and beliefs while many cannot even print their own names. What are some things you usually take for granted that are actually worth celebrating?

_____

_____

_____

_____

_____

_____

_____

_____

_____

_____

_____

_____

_____

_____

_____

_____

_____

Acceptance is acknowledging that a situation is what it is and giving yourself permission to struggle, to meet a challenging time as best you can and forgive yourself for any shortcomings without judgment.
—ELLEN HENDRIKSEN, PhD

What is a significant issue that you have not been able to resolve despite your best efforts? How can you accept it and move on?

_____

_____

_____

_____

_____

_____

_____

_____

_____

_____

_____

_____

_____

_____

It is within my power to either serve God or not to serve him. Serving him I add to my own good and the good of the whole world. Not serving him, I forfeit my own good and deprive the world of that good, which was in my power to create. —LEO TOLSTOY

What is at least one thing you can do to serve your Higher Power? How might this be beneficial to you and others?

_____

_____

_____

_____

_____

_____

_____

_____

_____

_____

_____

_____

_____

_____

_____

_____

Do you have an important untold story inside of you? If so, create a plan to share it.

_____

_____

_____

_____

_____

_____

_____

_____

_____

_____

_____

_____

_____

_____

_____

_____

The question of what you want to own is actually the question of how you want to live your life. —MARIE KONDO

What do you want to own and how does it reflect how you want to live your life?

_____

_____

_____

_____

_____

_____

_____

_____

_____

_____

_____

_____

_____

_____

_____

_____

_____

_____

A wheel was shown to me, wonderful to behold. . . . Divinity is in its omniscience and omnipotence like a wheel, a circle, a whole that can neither be understood, nor divided, nor begun nor ended. . . . God hugs you. You are encircled by the arms of the mystery of God. —HILDEGARD VON BINGEN

It is easy to believe that the world is spinning completely out of control, yet nature constantly proves that God remains in control. The night sky is one example—the cosmos is in perfect order. What in nature speaks to you of God's omnipresence and omnipotence?

DAY 343

Family is anyone who you can't imagine living without. —JENNIFER GARNER

Who can't you imagine living without and why?

I love sketching in Central Park because it helps me get in touch with nature. You realize when you're outside how beautiful the four seasons are and that the real artist is nature itself. —TONY BENNETT

What is your favorite way to connect to nature and why?

_____

_____

_____

_____

_____

_____

_____

_____

_____

_____

_____

_____

_____

_____

_____

_____

DAY 345

Evolution is a balancing act between sitting still and inching forward. I've heard a joke that even when you finally get yourself onto the right path, you will get run over if you don't keep moving. So we must treat each experience as a stepping stone, not a final destination. —TIMBER HAWKEYE

What stepping-stones are you using to reach an important goal?

Deep questions that arise naturally in the process of life's unfolding signal the manifestation of the very energy through which we grow further. We would be arrogant to believe that we can proceed far without pondering the important questions life asks of us. —AJAHN SUMANO BHIKKHU

Which important questions is life asking you now and what are your answers?

_____

_____

_____

_____

_____

_____

_____

_____

_____

_____

_____

_____

_____

_____

_____

_____

_____

DAY 347

Every step grows
The top of the mountain.
And sometimes the next step is
The hole through
The clouds beyond what
We know can hold us. And so we
Willingly
To outside ourselves
Go walking. —LAURA HOPE-GILL

What is the most recent thing you have done that took you out of your comfort zone? What did you gain from the experience?

_____

_____

_____

_____

_____

_____

_____

_____

_____

_____

_____

_____

_____

We can always opt to focus on that part of ourselves that is not made of thoughts, feelings, or bodily sensations. We can choose to focus on that space behind our thoughts—on the silence from which we observe ourselves and the world and the space that we keep forgetting to notice. —JUDITH LASATER, PhD

Meditational breathing is both a simple and effective way to connect to that peaceful space.

Find a place where you will be undisturbed for at least ten minutes. Sit or lie in a comfortable position, close your eyes, and begin slowly breathing in and out fully. While inhaling, mentally repeat the word "inhale" and repeat "exhale" with each exhalation. When thoughts, feelings, or bodily sensations arise, just note them in your awareness and return your attention to your breathing. Upon completing this meditation, journal about its effect.

DAY
349

If we did all the things we are capable of, we would literally astound ourselves. —THOMAS EDISON

Remember a time that you astounded yourself by doing something you thought was beyond your limits. What insight did you gain from this experience?

_____

_____

_____

_____

_____

_____

_____

_____

_____

_____

_____

_____

_____

_____

_____

_____

Certain things in life are so precious, so divinely perfect and sacred, that they don't need any alterations. They arise from the compassionate and boundless Existence, touch our hearts, and return to that placeless place where nothing ever repeats, leaving us in awe and wonder. Such perennial pearls of wisdom invite us to wholeness. For me, Rumi's teachings and poetry are some of those precious gifts in life. —POURIA MONTAZERI

Which perennial pearls of wisdom invite you to wholeness and how?

DAY
351

Though we rightfully feel the rip and pull of everything taken away from us, being stripped of what covers us helps us grow—by lightening our load and making us more raw and naked, so we can be touched and transformed by the elements of life. —MARK NEPO

Have you ever been stripped of your protective covering? What happened as a result?

_____

_____

_____

_____

_____

_____

_____

_____

_____

_____

_____

_____

_____

_____

_____

_____

_____

Follow your bliss, my go-to mantra, anchors me in a flow state where I'm super creative and feel so much appreciation for life itself—unexpected, amazing things happen! —RENAE

What is your go-to mantra and why?

_____

_____

_____

_____

_____

_____

_____

_____

_____

_____

_____

_____

_____

_____

I am a huge believer in luck, but more than that, that you can put yourself in the way of luck. It's like, if you're waiting for a bus, it sure as hell helps to be waiting at a bus stop. —ERIK LARSON

Few significant goals are reached by pure luck. Most require intentional, diligent steps. What steps are you taking to improve the quality of your life? If you haven't made any yet, use the space below to detail an action plan to do so.

_____

_____

_____

_____

_____

_____

_____

_____

_____

_____

_____

_____

_____

_____

_____

_____

_____

Do your work, then step back.
The only path to serenity. —LAO TZU

Remember the most recent time you did your best, then let go of the results.
How did you do that and how can you continue to do so?

_____

_____

_____

_____

_____

_____

_____

_____

_____

_____

_____

_____

_____

_____

_____

_____

_____

DAY
355

Practice scanning your body with the light of mindfulness and smiling to each part of your body with compassion and concern. —THICH NHAT HANH

Find a place where you can lie or sit comfortably. While breathing mindfully and smiling, direct loving-kindness first to your head. Allow it to radiate there like a warm light. Let the loving-kindness flow to your neck and shoulders, then slowly down the rest of your body. Rest in this position for a few more moments, then journal how you feel.

We want to do enormous stuff, stuff that Spielberg might be able to pull off, maybe. We don't want to do some tiny thing, some little shard in the mosaic. We want to do the whole panoramic portrait and it overwhelms us and totally thwarts us. The only way to approach it is in small bits. —ANNE LAMOTT

How can you break down a major task you need to do into smaller, more manageable parts?

_____

_____

_____

_____

_____

_____

_____

_____

_____

_____

_____

_____

_____

_____

_____

_____

DAY 357

Freedom is not worth having if it does not include the freedom to make mistakes. —MOHANDAS K. GANDHI

What is a recent mistake you made that offered an important lesson?

_____

_____

_____

_____

_____

_____

_____

_____

_____

_____

_____

_____

_____

_____

_____

_____

_____

_____

_____

_____

The degree of identification with the mind differs from person to person. Some people enjoy periods of freedom from it, however brief, and the peace, joy, and aliveness they experience in those moments make life worth living. —ECKHART TOLLE

How do you free yourself from your mind? How might you do this more often?

DAY
359

*Over the course of my lifetime, books have helped me know that I'm
not alone, even when I'm at my loneliest. They've given me the words to
articulate what I held in my heart but could not express.* —OPRAH WINFREY

Which books have comforted you during hard times and how did they do that?

_____

_____

_____

_____

_____

_____

_____

_____

_____

_____

_____

_____

_____

_____

_____

_____

_____

_____

_____

If I'm in a place where a dark cloud creeps over me and I can't shake it, I'll list five things I'm grateful for. It could be anything from "I'm grateful for my legs because I can walk and run" to "I'm grateful for that delicious breakfast I just had." When I've done that, I've never experienced a time that the grayness hasn't lifted. —ALICIA KEYS

List five things you are grateful for at this moment.

_____

_____

_____

_____

_____

_____

_____

_____

_____

_____

_____

_____

_____

_____

_____

_____

_____

_____

DAY
361

I feel that hanging out with my guitar and letting things come through, putting out the antenna and receiving things, is my form of meditation. —ANI DiFRANCO

What is your favorite form of meditation and why?

_____

_____

_____

_____

_____

_____

_____

_____

_____

_____

_____

_____

_____

_____

_____

_____

_____

_____

I'm 75 years old. It's a big number. The older I get, the more of myself I become. That's the beauty of being my age: You continue to step into being more and more of who you are. —GAIL PARKER, PhD

How are you stepping more into who you are? What helps you do this?

_____

_____

_____

_____

_____

_____

_____

_____

_____

_____

_____

_____

_____

_____

_____

_____

DAY 363

Instead of taking out loans to go to a school for the arts, maybe try to push yourself deeper into the world, to explore more bravely. Or go more deeply and bravely inward. Take an honest inventory of the education you already have—the years you have lived, the trials you have endured, the skills you have learned along the way. —ELIZABETH GILBERT

What are some of the most important skills you have learned thus far and how are you applying them?

_____

_____

_____

_____

_____

_____

_____

_____

_____

_____

_____

_____

_____

_____

_____

_____

For me, spirituality is always about honoring my dignity and always honoring the dignity of those around me. —REV. JES KAST

Detail how you most recently connected to your spirituality by honoring your dignity and that of someone else.

_____

_____

_____

_____

_____

_____

_____

_____

_____

_____

_____

_____

_____

_____

_____

_____

DAY
365

When lost in the gears of existence, we're always challenged to let in beauty while we're suffering, to let in love while we're struggling. What holds everything together, what releases resilience, and what renews us when we're struggling is relationship. Relationship is the lifeblood of inner health. —MARK NEPO

Who are the most significant people in your life and what is the quality of your relationships with them? How could you become closer?

_____

_____

_____

_____

_____

_____

_____

_____

_____

_____

_____

_____

_____

_____

_____

_____

_____

_____

_____

Follow-up Self-Assessment

To assess your current level of resilience, rate the following statements from 1 (strongly disagree) to 5 (strongly agree).

I cope well with frequent change.

| 1 | 2 | 3 | 4 | 5 |

I see problems as opportunities for personal growth.

| 1 | 2 | 3 | 4 | 5 |

It is easy for me to relax and focus on the present moment.

| 1 | 2 | 3 | 4 | 5 |

I am usually calm and centered.

| 1 | 2 | 3 | 4 | 5 |

I learn valuable lessons from every major setback I experience.

| 1 | 2 | 3 | 4 | 5 |

I meet most of the goals I set for myself.

| 1 | 2 | 3 | 4 | 5 |

I am a good problem solver.

| 1 | 2 | 3 | 4 | 5 |

I have a strong spiritual practice that helps keep me grounded.

| 1 | 2 | 3 | 4 | 5 |

I ask for help when I need it.

| 1 | 2 | 3 | 4 | 5 |

I seldom fret about things I cannot control.

| 1 | 2 | 3 | 4 | 5 |

I treat myself with compassion.

| 1 | 2 | 3 | 4 | 5 |

I can quickly do things differently based upon new information.

| 1 | 2 | 3 | 4 | 5 |

I avoid using alcohol or other chemical substances to cope with stress.

| 1 | 2 | 3 | 4 | 5 |

I set aside time daily to rest, meditate, and reflect.

| 1 | 2 | 3 | 4 | 5 |

I have very supportive family and friends.

| 1 | 2 | 3 | 4 | 5 |

When things go wrong in my life, I typically take responsibility instead of blaming others.

| 1 | 2 | 3 | 4 | 5 |

I seldom dwell on negative thoughts or emotions.

| 1 | 2 | 3 | 4 | 5 |

I exercise regularly and maintain a healthy diet.

1 | 2 | 3 | 4 | 5

I have the skills I need to accomplish important goals.

1 | 2 | 3 | 4 | 5

Insignificant things seldom bother me.

1 | 2 | 3 | 4 | 5

I have hobbies that add to the quality of my life.

1 | 2 | 3 | 4 | 5

I feel good about myself.

1 | 2 | 3 | 4 | 5

I frequently draw comfort from nature.

1 | 2 | 3 | 4 | 5

I can stand up for myself when people try to mistreat me.

1 | 2 | 3 | 4 | 5

I face challenges head-on instead of just wishing they would go away.

1 | 2 | 3 | 4 | 5

Notes

Credits

Copyright © 2022 by Sandra E. Johnson

Published in the United States by Clarkson Potter/Publishers,
an imprint of Random House, a division of
Penguin Random House LLC, New York.

ClarksonPotter.com
RandomHouseBooks.com

CLARKSON POTTER is a trademark and POTTER
with colophon is a registered trademark of
Penguin Random House LLC.

ISBN 978-0-593-23435-8

Printed in Malaysia

Editor: Lindley Boegehold
Designer: Nicole Block
Production Editor: Serena Wang
Production Manager: Luisa Francavilla
Composition: Merri Ann Morrell, Zoe Tokushige
Copy Editor: Tom Pitoniak

10 9 8 7 6 5 4 3 2 1

First Edition